THE REFERENCE SHELF *(Continued)*

Volume 23

No.
2. Representative American Speeches: 1950-1951. A. C. Baird. $1.75.

No.
6. Gambling in America. H. L. Marx, Jr. $1.75.

Volume 22

No. 3. Representative American Speeches: 1949-1950. A. C. Baird. $1.75.

Volume 21

No. 2. Representative American Speeches: 1948-1949. A. C. Baird. $1.75.

Volume 20

No.
5. Federal World Government. J. E. Johnsen. $1.50.

Volume 19

No. 3. Free Medical Care. C. A. Peters. $1.25.

Volume 18

No.
3. Representative American Speeches: 1944-1945. A. C. Baird. $1.25.

No.
6. Palestine: Jewish Homeland? J. E. Johnsen. $1.25.

Volume 17

No. 4. Representative American Speeches: 1943-1944. A. C. Baird. $1.25.

Volume 16

No.
1. Representative American Speeches: 1941-1942. A. C. Baird. $1.25.

No.
6. Representative American Speeches: 1942-1943. A. C. Baird. $1.25.

THE REFERENCE SHELF

Vol. 29   No. 2

DC409
D3

FRANCE IN CRISIS

Edited by
ELIZABETH DAVEY

THE H. W. WILSON COMPANY
NEW YORK   1957

PREFACE

It can be said at the outset that to compile a book of contemporary articles on France and come up with a unified, coherent whole is a difficult task. For the welter of recent writing about our complex ally is overwhelmingly concerned with why she is the way she is—a riddle to be solved or a patient to be psychoanalyzed. Nonetheless, from the very preoccupation of this writing emerges a central fact: that an understanding of France has been a continuing concern of American scholars, journalists, and statesmen. The reason for this is not hard to find: in a world sharply divided between the democracies and Communist totalitarianism, France can lay claim to having been a prime contributor to the democratic tradition. A study of the situation of modern France can give fresh insight into this tradition, its inherent weaknesses and its perennial strength. Another reason quite logically is that France is a key power, if not the key power, in democratic Western Europe.

The purpose of this book is to set forth representative current views on the present political situation of France, in the light of the more important developments since the end of World War II. For a fuller background on French affairs, the books listed in the bibliography at the end of this volume should be consulted. Several highly acclaimed, authoritative books on France have been published in recent years. Perhaps the most important of these is Herbert Luethy's *France Against Herself*.

It should be added that since this compilation is concerned with French political affairs, only incidental references are made to French cultural life, and comparatively little is said about France's economic problems.

Finally, in compiling this book, it has been difficult to keep pace with rapidly changing events. Some of the material included will inevitably show its dateline by the time of publication. It is hoped, however, that the essential aspects of the major problems confronting France have been covered and presented in such a way that the book will serve as a base for understanding what is to come.

The compiler wishes to thank the various authors and publishers who have granted permission for the use of materials included in this book. She would also like to thank Mr. Grant McClellan and Mr. Victor Velen for their very helpful suggestions on the content of the book.

ELIZABETH DAVEY

January 1957

CONTENTS

I. THE FRENCH POLITICAL SYSTEM

EDITOR'S INTRODUCTION

An American whose knowledge of France is limited to an occasional headline in the daily press is aware only of a pattern of seemingly constant governmental crisis, wherein one cabinet succeeds another with alarming frequency. A common saying among Americans in fact is: "The trouble with France is too much politics." Yet there are inner forces at work in the French democratic system that tend to counterbalance and stabilize the unstable forces. If this were not true, it would be difficult to see how the French so far have been able to keep their democracy intact and out of the hands of the extremists of Right and Left.

Most observers of the French scene select a particular facet of French political life to point to as the cause of all of France's ills. Frequent targets are: the absence of a balance of power between the executive and legislative branches of government (the supremacy of the French National Assembly); the multiparty system, in which no party can gain a stable majority to govern; an electoral law that tends to perpetuate the multiparty system; the large Communist vote in France that returns a substantial group of Communist deputies to the Assembly with every election; and, finally, the French character itself—the Frenchman's strong individualism, his general hostility to authority in any form, and his lack of civic responsibility. All of these arguments and more are presented in this section.

In the first article Professor Saul Padover gives some general views of the nature of the French problem at home and warns of its unfavorable consequences to the French position abroad. An article by Gordon Wright gives some psychological insights into the French political character. A distinguished French scholar, André Siegfried, discusses the results of the January 1956 elections in the light of the historical factors that motivate the French to vote as they do. In the subsequent article, news analyst Edgar Mowrer sets down his observations after an extensive tour of France and concludes that what France needs is an economic revolution. An article by Guy de Carmoy, a high-ranking French civil servant and professor at the Institute of Political Science in Paris, argues that the French crisis is a moral one. Another article by Gordon Wright takes up three important needs for reform: in the electoral law, in the Assembly's rules of conduct, and in the constitution itself. An article on the fall of the Mendès-France government demonstrates the dramatic impact of Mendèsism on the recent French scene. In the next article the *New Yorker's* old Paris hand, Janet Flanner ("Genêt"), comes strongly to the defense of the French at a time—just after the downfall of the Mendès-France government—when French prestige was at its lowest point since the end of World War II. Two dispatches by Harold Callender, chief of the New York *Times* Paris bureau, analyze the meaning of the Communist vote in France. An article by Harry L. Turtledove describes Poujadism, a thorny recent problem on the French Right. Finally, C. L. Sulzberger, New York *Times* roving correspondent, writes of de Gaulle in retirement and the wane of Gaullism as a political force.

TIME IS RUNNING OUT FOR FRANCE [1]

It is now abundantly clear that France is a chronically sick country. Its malaise is less of the body than of the spirit. For physically there is nothing wrong with France. Its birth rate is rising. Its economy is improving steadily. Industrial output is higher than before 1939. Electric power and steel production have reached new records. Agriculture is being mechanized to a point where there is a considerable food surplus. Resources and soil are still rich and undepleted. The body of France, in short, is in good shape.

What, then, is wrong with France? In essence, the root of France's trouble lies in the lack of that spirit for which the French have a fine word—namely, *civisme*: the sense of citizenship, with all its duties, obligations, civic responsibility and community cooperation. This spirit has long been lacking in France, a country whose people are primarily individualistic and only secondarily civic-minded. Not only is the Frenchman traditionally an individualist—he is also instinctively suspicious of the state.

The Frenchman is particularly wary of a strong government, which, he knows from past experience, has nearly always been tyrannical, oppressive and costly. Louis XIV and Napoleon are the most conspicuous examples of such heavy-handed governments; but there have been many others, less brilliant but equally burdensome. Acting on the principle that all government is bad but a weak one is best, the French have swung from iron-fisted Bourbonism and Bonapartism to the other extreme.

As a result, in recent decades France has been in a state of chronic political crisis. The current Fourth

[1] From "France in Crisis," by Saul K. Padover, dean of the School of Politics, New School for Social Research, New York. *Foreign Policy Bulletin.* 35:49-50. December 15, 1955. Reprinted by permission.

Republic, whose constitution was adopted in 1946, is the product of the national character and historic experience. As such, it contains deliberately-built-in mechanisms that make strong and effective government all but impossible. This was the reason why General de Gaulle, chief of state when the constitution came into force, resigned rather than serve a government that was born crippled.

In a way, the French may be said to be suffering from too much democracy: every shade of opinion is represented in parliament; every special interest is given a potent voice. Hence no one or two or even three parties can preponderate. The formation of a government requires a temporary coalition of several parties and blocs. . . . France's president, now René Coty, is but a figurehead with even less power than is possessed by the British monarch. The premier . . . is at the mercy of parliamentary cliques and temporary combinations. There is, in short, no effective central authority, and under the constitution there can never be any. . . .

France could continue to rock along on its present path if there were no international and colonial crises. At home the civil service and the permanent under-secretaries in the various ministries could manage the government, as they have done hitherto. But foreign affairs and an inflamed colonial situation, notably in North Africa, require long-range planning, continuity of policy and bold action. These are at present lacking in France. Here is the root of the trouble, not only for France but for the whole free world.

The instability of its governments has gravely reduced France's prestige abroad. The Germans, accustomed as they are to authority and discipline, have been developing anew a kind of disrespect for a disunited and seemingly chaotic France. This may have unfortunate repercussions in foreign policy. Already the Saarlanders, ethnically and linguistically German, voted on October 23, 1955, against France, despite the fact that the Saar's economic union with France has brought them prosperity.

Worst of all has been France's colonial problem. In the absence of a durable and vigorous executive it has been extremely difficult to reach wise and long-range colonial decisions. In 1954, after Premier Mendès-France had worked out a firm policy for North Africa, he was literally hooted out of office by an enraged and irresponsible parliament. Crises in the French colonies have been going from bad to worse and, in the case of Indo-China, even to defeat and disaster. Irresponsibility and lack of decision in Paris are gradually undermining France's colonial empire, the second greatest in the world.

All these developments have an important effect on the foreign policy of the United States, particularly with regard to NATO. Both strategically and militarily NATO has been hinged on France and its North African possessions. But the recent violent uprisings in . . . Algeria, a department of France, have forced Paris to transfer a part of its best troops to North Africa, with the result that NATO has been seriously weakened. This leaves a gap in NATO which the West may be unable to fill.

In this situation there is not much the United States can do, except exert constant moral and diplomatic pressure on the more responsible French politicians to develop vigorously an effective and forward-looking North African policy. It is now too late for half measures. In spite of recent improvements the North Africans, over the long run, will probably not be satisfied with anything less than independence. This should be promised them in the foreseeable future, and the United States should guarantee that the promise will be carried out, with due

regard to the security and livelihood of 2 million Frenchmen settled in North Africa. Such a policy would not
only save France from a kind of slow hemorrhage in
North Africa but would also create in that strategic area
an important group of friends for the free world.

A NEW LOOK AT AN OLD ALLY [2]

France, we may as well admit, does not attract un-
mixed esteem and admiration in this country. Adjectives
like "sick," "demoralized," and "decadent" roll off the
tongue or the pen with dismaying frequency and glibness.
Editorialists complain that "France . . . cannot be counted
upon as a firm member of the Atlantic alliance.". . . A
visitor from the Orient might wonder at times whether
France is an ally or an enemy—until he recalls that nations often reserve their most thoughtless recrimination
and abuse for their allies. . . .

Marianne, France's chosen symbol, is a woman. Now
feminine subjects are notoriously difficult of analysis;
they are by tradition complex, often unpredictable, at
once fascinating and irritating. Ambrose Bierce remarked on one occasion that for a study of the good and
bad in woman, two women are a needless expense. So
it is with France: the good and the bad, the strong and
the weak points are hopelessly intertwined.

It is always tempting in the feminine realm to dwell
upon the frailties rather than the factors of strength.
Forever Amber might have won fewer readers if Amber's better nature had more often triumphed. In the
case of France, the temptation is especially great because
the weaknesses appear to be so flagrant. Politically, the
nation seems to stagger dizzily from one cabinet crisis to

[2] From "A New Look at An Old Ally: The State of France," by Gordon
Wright, professor of history, University of Oregon. *Virginia Quarterly Review.*
29:321-38. Summer 1953. Reprinted by permission.

another. Socially, there are stresses and strains which
lead every segment of society—farmers, workers, businessmen—to feel sorry for itself and bitter toward all
other segments. In economics, a kind of chronic stag-
nancy has kept French production and living standards
from ever rising very far above the 1913 level. Militarily,
there is the painful effort to build up fifteen divisions of
French troops in Europe, whereas not so long ago there
were more than a hundred. Morally, one can point to that
lack of civic spirit or self-discipline which irritates Anglo-
Saxons so much, and which deeply disturbs many Frenchmen as well. And on top of all these failings, there is the
fact that in . . . [North Africa and elsewhere] France is
currently the custodian of some of the prickliest problems
of the Western world. Here indeed, it might seem, is
the ideal soft spot for Stalin to drive his new wedge
into the Western coalition.

It is easy to point out what is wrong with France. It
is much more difficult to counterbalance this with what
is right. Since the war, the French have produced some
of the ablest leaders and some of the most fertile ideas
of any Western nation. Few countries have a democratic
tradition that is more genuine or more deeply rooted.
The texture of society, while subject to serious stresses
and strains, seems resilient enough to resist all but a major
shock. Yet these things are amorphous and hard to
measure, let alone to prove. Perhaps their validity will
have to be accepted in part on faith, intuitively rather
than "scientifically." Both the past and the future, I
think, will justify that faith.

Three Traits

Any attempt to psychoanalyze a nation is a risky
business. Indeed, Sam Goldwyn once remarked that anybody who goes to a psychiatrist ought to have his head

examined. While admitting the danger, it seems appropriate to comment briefly on three French traits or habits of thought which may throw some light on the institutions and the behavior of our oldest ally.

France, someone has observed, is the only country in the world where the good citizen is the one who resists authority. This resistance does not grow out of sheer perversity or a morbid desire for self-expression; it is a matter of principle. The political essayist who called himself Alain wrote some years ago: "Obey, but resist; there is the whole secret. Without obedience, you have anarchy; but without resistance, you have tyranny." French democracy grew up and formulated its doctrines in an era when authority was repressive and hostile. Repeated interludes of authoritarian government have ingrained the habit deeply. This defiance of authority goes far to explain not only the Frenchman's preference for crossing streets on red lights, but also his suspicion of a strong executive power and his legendary efforts to beat the tax collector. One curious manifestation of it was the squabble in 1951 between the taxi drivers of Paris and the police. The chauffeurs, ordered to submit to a medical examination, threatened to block this invasion of their liberties by obeying all Paris traffic laws for a full day. The police, replying in the same spirit, warned that they would revoke the driver's license of any chauffeur guilty of such un-French behavior.

One can find similar reflections of this anti-authoritarian trait in political life. There is in southern France a widespread tradition of voting for the most radical party as the one most likely to oppose the government. The theory is that any government is innately suspect, and needs to be harassed as much as possible. The eminent French political analyst François Goguel tells of a fellow-traveling southern villager who, after the liberation of France in 1944, won election as mayor at the head of the Communist ticket. Some months later, the mayor remarked to a friend from Paris: "You know, these Communists are getting too strong in France; something has got to be done." "But, *mon Dieu!*" exploded the friend; "look at yourself; didn't you and all your friends vote Communist?" "Yes, of course," admitted the mayor, "but we didn't vote for them to put them in power."

No doubt the prevalence of this trait can be overstressed. Many Frenchmen do not share it; but it does go deep in Frenchmen of the political Center, and it does help to explain some aspects of French political life. Like so many French traits, it combines both good and bad: the defense of the individual and his rights on the one hand, a weakening of society as a whole on the other. Someone has said that in a healthy democracy there must be a balance between the forces of individualism and the forces of social cohesion. The French, it seems clear, have tilted the balance too much one way. How to restore equilibrium without tilting it even farther the other way is a grave issue in this epoch of crisis.

A second deep-rooted trait is the strain of skepticism so often found in French minds. Perhaps this factor is related to the first one; in any case, it is another of those ambivalent qualities with contradictory effects. At its best, this skepticism creates in Frenchmen a healthy resistance to political crusades—to those fanatics whose nostrums must be swallowed blindly in order to be enjoyed. But at its worst, this trait can inspire a cynicism and a rejection of all values which strike at the roots of any society. There are times, perhaps, when even democracies need a touch of the crusading temper to survive.

The third characteristic is what David Thomson has called the Frenchman's habit of historical thinking. In this age of super-powers, we sometimes forget that France has a long history as a great power and as a cultural leader: a history that has lasted down into our own day, at least in appearance. And since it is true that Frenchmen are inclined to look backward, to think of the present in terms of the past, it is especially difficult for them to adjust to this new age. One Frenchman wrote a century ago: "For a nation which has once known greatness, there can be no middle ground between power and slavery." Some of his countrymen—notably Charles de Gaulle—agree that there is no middle ground; that France can and must be a great power once again, because the only alternative is a kind of slavery. . . .

The habit of historical thinking can, as Arnold Toynbee points out, degenerate into archaism—into an attempt to restore past greatness by repeating past phrases and gestures. Yet here again, this French trait can be a factor of strength. From the habit of historical thinking, a nation ought to derive a degree of balance and perspective, of insight and wisdom, which younger and more contemporary-minded nations may sometimes lack. One cannot be sure that France's role as teacher and philosopher is ended.

The Political System

From psychoanalysis, let us turn now to anatomy: to the functioning political-social-economic organism that is France.

It is rather depressing that a nation with so old and deep a democratic tradition has always had so much trouble in making democracy work. Wiseacres suggest that the Tunisians are beginning to ask whether the

French are ready for self-government. Such a view is somewhat extreme; and the French might answer, as did the owner of the Brooklyn Dodgers, "Half the lies they tell about us ain't true." It is worth pointing out that French political leaders in the past decade have shown a notable degree of originality and adaptability. It is fair to add, too, that in the . . . eight years [following the liberation] (except for one brief month) there . . . [were] only two different Foreign Ministers in France, and that both of them came from the same party. This is a record of stability and consistency which few nations can equal, and which hardly squares with popular ideas about French political fickleness.

The fact remains that the French do not possess the political scientist's ideal of government. Their system is better designed to prevent things from being done than it is to get things done. This is traceable in part to the constitution, with its weak executive; in part to the political habits and mores of the French; and in part to the balance of political forces in the National Assembly. . . .

Let us look first at the two extremes of Left and Right. The Communists can still boast with justice that their party is the largest one in France. Its élite, its hard core, is tough and disciplined, with more than the normal French measure of dynamism, faith, and certainty. Its organizational structure is tighter and far more elaborate than that of any other French party. Its strength, as measured by voting support rather than by party membership, is more widely distributed both geographically and sociologically than that of any rival group. . . .

The curve of Gaullist strength, unlike that of Communism, has fluctuated widely in the past few years. Second among parties in the 1951 elections, first in its parliamentary representation, . . . [Charles de Gaulle's

Rassemblement du Peuple Français, or People's Rally]
has more recently undergone a series of seismic shocks
which have split both its élite and its popular following.
These ups and downs were the almost inevitable product
of the movement's inner contradictions. Organized
Gaullism never approached a monolithic unity. Alongside
the ardent disciples, there were some self-seeking op-
portunists and many conservative hitch-hikers. These
semi-Gaullist conservatives asked nothing better than a
safe and sane alternative to Gaullism; and when men like
Antoine Pinay and René Mayer offered them such an
alternative, they left the Rally in droves. De Gaulle's
retort in May 1953 was to withdraw the remnants of his
movement from the foul air of parliamentary politics,
and to assign to the Rally a higher and presumably purer
mission. As "an advance guard for regrouping the people
to change the regime," it will henceforth save its strength
for a future crisis when, in de Gaulle's words, "once
again the supreme law would be the salvation of the
country and the state." . . .

What, then, of the Center? Here the task of analysis
becomes at the same time less colorful and more difficult.
Yet for any study of France today, this part of the
examination is of prime importance; for in the hands of
the Center rests the fate of the Fourth Republic.

Party lines divide the Center into five or six different
groups. The most meaningful line of separation, however, is the almost indefinable one which distinguishes
Left Center from Right Center: the former New Dealish
in temperament, the latter professedly liberal in the old-
fashioned meaning of that term. On the face of it, these
two groups are about evenly balanced both in the nation
at large and in parliament. But in fact the Right Center
is dominant today, and the cards seem plainly stacked in
its favor.

This generalization, if valid, has some profound implications for France both today and tomorrow. To explain and justify it, a brief venture into the fringes of sociology and economics is essential. Essayists have often sought to explain the French by arguing that there are two Frances: the urban and the rural, or the Red and the Black, or the party of Movement and the party of Established Order. Of all such dichotomies, however, the most significant is the one which François Goguel has recently propounded under the labels "dynamic France" and "static France."

In a sense, France straddles the nineteenth and the twentieth centuries. Great areas and great segments of the population are still archaic in their techniques and in their psychology: the small peasants, the artisans, the shopkeepers. This static France has changed little since the days of Louis Philippe. But superimposed upon it is dynamic France, made up of modernized factories (some of them very large), big mechanized farms, and some small but efficient and highly specialized farms.

The economic center of gravity in France today is in dynamic France. There lies the bulk of the nation's production and wealth. But the political center of gravity remains in static France, which is slightly more populous and enjoys an even greater advantage in parliamentary representation. Here, it would seem, is the most important key to an understanding of modern France's chronic crisis. Recent elections show clearly that the voters of dynamic France have been swinging toward the political extremes of Right and Left, while static France remains more faithful to the democratic Center parties which run the government. This growing dependence on static France is most characteristic of the Right Center, whose whole leadership is rooted in and made up of the "small" Frenchmen from town and village. But it is becoming increasingly characteristic of the Left Center as well—of the New Dealish Socialists and Christian Socialists. . . .

There are grave implications in this state of things. Static France is allergic to change. It is morbidly suspicious of dynamic experiments in modernization which may benefit—but may also destroy—the static sector. Static France wants a weak and cheap government that keeps taxes low, that avoids planning, that stays out of wars. If static France aimed at real laissez-faire in the sense of a free competitive economy, much might be said for its position. But this is not what it wants. Rather, static France clings to the ideal of a little man's protective association, aimed against its big domestic rivals and its foreign competitors. And this latter ideal, by and large, is what France has attained today. Successive governments have jettisoned the controls of the war and reconstruction period, waving the banner of liberalism and free enterprise. But behind those controls there have reappeared the old prewar controls: tariffs, anti-chain-store laws, domestic price-fixing agreements, special arrangements to protect certain rickety segments of the economy. In short, there exists once more a kind of barbed-wire entanglement protecting static France.

These, then, are the citizens who back the Center parties. Their influence makes it almost impossible for any Center coalition to push ahead vigorously toward reform and modernization. Most of the Right Center leaders don't want to do so. The Left Center leaders may want to, but they hesitate to offend those voters who now make up about half their support. Nor is it likely that any Center coalition can be stable and durable; for each of these parties must seek to outbid the others in competing for the same clientele. . . .

Marianne, as has been noted earlier, is a woman. Perhaps that is why Americans vary so widely in their estimates of France; for cool objectivity on feminine subjects is hard to attain. Some of us are inclined to love them no matter how great their faults; others are instinctively hostile and suspicious; still others merely admit our bafflement. If we must insist on perfection in our allies, we may as well admit that France falls well short of that standard. But on a relative scale, compared to other potential allies in this imperfect world of ours, there are few nations in the same class.

If this premise can be granted, then it follows that we had better be prepared to take France as she is, the bad with the good, with all her lapses and imperfections. For there seems little prospect of any drastic major improvement in our time, whether it be in the political, the social, the economic, or even the tax-collecting realm. Those Frenchmen who are peddling nostrums for the nation's ills are not likely to have a chance to try out their schemes. For that matter, most of those schemes would probably do more harm than good. Such advances as France does make in our time will come gradually, through an evolution so slow that only retrospect will make us clearly aware of them. But with luck, there can be such progress in France: progress toward greater stability in politics, toward more vigor in economic life, toward a healthier morale. And gains of this sort can mean the survival of one of the few deep-rooted democracies in the twentieth-century world.

Frenchmen like to point out that they have contributed as much as any nation to the basic ideology of the Western world—that ideology which is one of our principal weapons against Stalinism. It is true that in practice French concepts and qualities are better adapted to quiet times than to a period of stress. Most Frenchmen lack the tough, fanatical conviction that they possess the truth and are ready to die for it. They are not apt to be fanatically united about anything. But perhaps it is just as well that there are still some nations which lack that dangerous sense of infallibility. Unless, of course, we have already crossed a watershed of history into a new age—an age when tolerance can no longer be tolerated, when government by argument is out of date, and when it cannot safely be held that one man's ideas are as good as another's or a little bit better. If that age is upon us, then indeed it is time for Frenchmen to become extinct.

THE PRECARIOUS POLITICAL BALANCE IN FRANCE [3]

It must always be remembered that the Frenchman, the man in the street as well as the intellectual, is above all an individualist. But, it may be argued, there are individualists everywhere; this is scarcely a Gallic monopoly. The answer is that the individualism of the Frenchman is Latin in essence, which means that he has a capacity for stating problems clearly and for seeing in any solution the principle involved and the direction in which it leads. This quality of mind, admirable in itself, becomes a serious liability in politics, since it prevents ready adjustment by compromise. Every argument becomes a matter of principle; the practical results are relegated to second place. Further, since every Frenchman has his own individual outlook, there naturally must be a great number of political parties. A simple yes or no answer does not satisfy the French. This means that each party inevitably develops within itself a Left, Center

[3] From "Stable Instability in France," by André Siegfried, French authority on the United States and until recently professor at the Collège de France. *Foreign Affairs.* 34:394-404. April 1956. Reprinted by permission. Copyright by the Council on Foreign Relations, Inc.

and Right faction. As a result, government can function only through coalitions, and these are especially precarious because they are founded on such subtle combinations. Thus the means often obscures the ends. I should like to point out that this political game is intelligent; contrary to what superficial observers might believe, if it can be called politically intelligent to separate intelligence from effectiveness. As to all this the French are held to be blithely indifferent, ready to sacrifice practical considerations for a principle even when expediency counsels the opposite. From this point of view French politics certainly are interesting; speaking for myself, I wish they were less so.

History seems to have aggravated the conditions in which France chooses her leaders and formulates her basic political ideas regarding authority and freedom. Indeed, from the time the Revolution posed this fundamental dilemma France has never succeeded in resolving it. The reason is that she won democracy and freedom through a long struggle against reactionary regimes which only in the last extremity would acknowledge the sovereignty of the people, the supremacy of the elected assemblies and the complete secularization of the state. This struggle has produced a democratic tradition which will admit that only the elected assemblies truly represent the popular will. The French Left thus inclines to suspect that any administration which governs with authority is reactionary; it fails to distinguish clearly between arbitrary rule, discredited by its abuses, and the authority essential for governing at all. Even necessary restraints upon freedom are accepted reluctantly. . . .

Because the French mind senses political orientations so easily—almost instinctively—it naturally considers that concepts of Right and Left have essential significance. Democracy triumphed through the Left; reaction is expressed through the Right. . . . The French see everything in terms of a watershed, the two sides of which slant away so steeply that one cannot maintain a foothold at the top but must necessarily fall down on one side or the other. The terms "Right" and "Left," which do not mean much to Anglo-Saxon Americans, have dynamic and passionate force in France; they contain the threat of a return to the past, the promise of the future. The concept of the Left as cherished by its militant adherents is singular, almost childlike, akin to what inspires a Moslem as he looks toward Mecca. It is a rule of faith with them always to vote Left; in fact, they believe that the further to the Left they are the most effectively they will be resisting reaction. No one, not even the Rightist, wants to be considered to be on the Right. . . .

France thus is burdened with the weight of her past, and the burden is the heavier because that past has never been entirely resigned to being extinguished but every once in a while crops up again, if not in its earlier form, then in a new one. In 1940, for example, Marshal Pétain, in his "National Revolution," called to his aid the most reactionary traditions in our history. In 1945, when France faced the task of drawing up a constitution, this recent experience was bound to weigh heavily in the decisions that had to be made. Is it any wonder so many ghosts haunted the men who were striving to establish a Fourth Republic?

The Constitution of 1946, the charter of the Fourth Republic, reflects all these anxieties. Since it was the work of a Leftist majority it provided for a National Assembly elected by universal suffrage and with virtually unlimited powers. The cabinet was to be simply its delegate, always subject to dismissal. This was indeed the parliamentary regime in the democratic tradition of 1793, where the elected deputy is the sole true representative of the people. Chosen by the sovereign power, the deputy soon comes to believe that he himself is that power, so much so that he considers it little short of a scandal if an appeal is made to his constituents to revoke the mandate they have given him.

If in 1945 the Communists who then formed part of the majority coalition had had their way, there would have been no President of the Republic and no second chamber, only the single Assembly without any counterbalance, and the cabinet would have been merely its executive committee. When the referendum of May 1946 demonstrated the public's preference for a system which put certain restraints on the power of the Assembly, it was agreed that there should be a President of the Republic and a second chamber, the Council of the Republic. But the spirit of the Constitution was such that these modifications did not seriously affect the dominance of the National Assembly. The Council of the Republic, with only the negligible power of a suspensive veto, in no way corresponded to the Senate of the previous regime, and the prerogatives of the President of the Republic were jealously limited. A strong executive able to counterbalance the power of the National Assembly was not wanted. Thus France deliberately turned her back on the type of presidential regime favored by General de Gaulle. Even though the Leftist majority was drawn almost entirely from the ranks of the Resistance, it feared a possible dictator in the person of the liberator himself. . . .

Professor Philip Williams in his *Politics in Post-War France,* the best book on the Fourth Republic, calls attention to the similarity between this Constitution and the

English system with its all-powerful House of Commons, its king who reigns but does not rule and its House of Lords which has virtually no real prerogatives. These institutions have brought England ministerial stability and stable parties. How is it, then, that analogous institutions in France produce exactly the opposite result? The explanation of this is in part psychological, in part due to a difference in circumstances.

Take, for example, the multiplicity of French parties which is so often the cause of reproach. The difficulty is that too many questions of fundamental importance on which the various parties have cause to disagree have come up for decision at one time. The nineteenth century bequeathed to us the problem of *dirigisme* [state guidance of industry] versus free enterprise and that of separation of Church and State. Problems more urgent still, most of them resulting from the Second World War, now have us by the throat: European integration, German rearmament, the pro-Russian or pro-American orientation of our foreign policy, the colonial crisis. The fact that these problems, distinct in themselves, have arisen simultaneously increases the difficulty of forming a stable majority. A majority can be found on each of these problems taken singly—EDC [European Defense Community], for example, or the separation of Church and State—but when it comes to obtaining a majority which will agree on all these questions at once the task becomes truly formidable. Yet this is just what must be done if the cabinet is to reach decisions binding upon all its members, representing different parties in the coalition. The Socialists and Popular Republicans may agree on a social program, but the Socialists oppose the subsidies for Catholic schools sponsored by the Popular Republicans. Gaullists and Catholics may be together on the school question, but not on the question of European integration.

Such divisions are in large part responsible for the cabinet instability which has become tragically characteristic of the French parliamentary regime. Unfortunately this instability follows logically from the circumstances described above. The moment the cabinet is considered the delegate of the Assembly majority, any change in the center of gravity or composition of that majority necessarily involves a cabinet shake-up. The process is a little like the way a skipper trims his sails as the wind changes. If the cabinet is not overthrown it comes apart; certain ministers refuse to associate themselves with some measure they do not approve. Actually the disadvantages are not as serious as they appear to foreign observers. When there is a cabinet crisis, certain ministers change or the same ministers are merely shifted around; but no civil servant is displaced, and the day-by-day administration continues without interruption. Furthermore, as the same ministers hold over from one cabinet to another, they form as it were teams of government. This leads to the paradox of stable policy with unstable cabinets. Our international critics nevertheless have a strong point when they complain that the representatives of France in diplomatic negotiations are hardly ever the same from one year to the next.

How, despite such a capricious regime, does France survive and even prosper (for she is not in a state of crisis)? To understand it, one must remember that two parallel traditions have been maintained since the eighteenth century: a political tradition characterized by constant variations and affirmations of principle without fundamental regard for practical effects; and an administrative tradition originating with Napoleon characterized by permanence and solidity. The two do not obey the same rules or the same spirit, but the second is no less national than the first.

In spite of all this French politics do not lack continuity. If instead of considering each cabinet individually one classifies them by groups having the same general complexion, one begins to discern periods of continuity which to a certain extent counterbalance the instability of the separate cabinets. Since the Liberation there have been three such periods. During the first, from 1944 to 1947, the majorities were based on the cooperation of the Communists, Socialists and Popular Republicans (Catholic Left). When Ramadier excluded the Communists in May 1947, a new tripartite regime was formed, more toward the Center this time, embracing the Socialists, Popular Republicans and Radicals. The electoral system of 1951 was devised in order to consolidate this combination against both communism and Gaullism. The system must be understood if the results of the 1956 elections, held under the same rules, are to be interpreted correctly.

Under this system, all seats go to the ticket winning 51 per cent of the votes in a department or section of a department. If no party wins a majority, the seats are distributed among all parties in proportion to the number of votes received by each. However, if two or three parties declare that although they are retaining their separate identities they are forming an electoral alliance, they are considered as a single party for the purposes of the election and are allowed all the seats if their pooled votes total more than 50 per cent of the votes cast. This system puts a premium on cooperation between parties and works against isolated parties. . . .

Despite the existence of a strong Gaullist element to the Right, the tripartite majority regime, based on the Center, could have maintained itself in power after the 1951 elections if the question of subsidies to the Catholic schools had not arisen to separate the Socialists from the Popular Republicans. This made it necessary for a governing majority to look for support further to the Right, even to the Gaullists; and this in turn drove the Socialists toward the Left and revived the idea of a popular front. But any alliance between parties as different as the Independents on the Right and the Popular Republicans, socially oriented toward the Left, was bound to be precarious, the more so because they were not in agreement on the problem of Europe and German rearmament, just then coming to the fore. Governmental instability increased, but suddenly two circumstances cleared the air. For one thing, prices, which had been rising constantly for ten years, began with the Pinay regime in 1953 to be stabilized, while American and European prosperity began to be reflected in the French economy. For another, the strong personality of Mendès-France emerged, and he assumed leadership of a new majority oriented toward the Left. But could a Left majority be constituted without the aid of the Communists, or a Center majority without the Socialists and the Radicals who follow Mendès-France? A split ensued in the Center of the Assembly between the parties and the leaders—Mendès-France and Edgar Faure—who had lately been cooperating. Faure called for the dissolution of the Assembly in December 1955, hoping to obtain clear guidance from the people as to the direction in which French policy should move. But as the dissolution took place without any change having been made in the electoral system, and as no alliance was made among the deeply divided Center parties, the seats were distributed proportionately.

Under the system as it functioned in the 1956 elections, the voter cast his vote less for individuals than for parties. This abstract concept may be pleasing to the French mind, but it separates the voter from reality. As a result, the balloting was more like a census than an election. On the essential issues the electorate did not give any clear indication of its opinion.

Three spectacular results demand attention: the gain of some 50 seats by the Communists (their number rose from 95 to 144); the sudden eruption onto the scene of 51 Poujadist deputies on the extreme Right [see "The New Face of the French Right," in this section, below— Ed.]; and the adoption of an intransigent position by the Republican Front, which chose to place itself on the Left side of the watershed, in opposition to the former majority of Edgar Faure. These results will appear less startling to foreign observers if they will recall the analysis presented earlier in this article. Once again the French have been true to their traditional psychology; no really new currents have appeared. It would be too much to draw from this election any definite conclusions as to French tendencies, whether reassuring or otherwise. From the point of view of public opinion, no clear-cut indications appear. However, from the tactical and governmental point of view, the new distribution, not of votes but of seats, raises difficult problems. . . .

Even if they do not know exactly what they want, fifty Poujadist deputies can, by joining their votes to those of the Communists, increase the difficulty of constituting a parliamentary majority.

France has always suffered from extreme Leftist and Rightist minorities which do not participate in good faith in the exercise of republican government. To constitute a majority with the aid of the Communists would be to resurrect the Popular Front, a mortal peril to the Republic, as Socialists and Radicals are well aware. But to constitute a majority with the aid of untrustworthy elements on the extreme Right would only encourage the formation of just such a popular front under the false pretense of "defending the Republic." This is to be feared above all else. Numerically the Center commands a majority, exclusive of Communists and Poujadists. The partisan and personal rivalries which separate the Republican Front from the groups in the Center and on the liberal Right make the consolidation of this majority very difficult. Yet the exigencies of a situation which is serious to the point of real danger make it imperative.

FRANCE'S ECONOMIC MALAISE [4]

"We just can't go on like this," Burgundy wine-grower Maurice Pavelot, of Pernand Vergelesses, told me over a well-loaded lunch table. "Something has to change here," echoed Rodolphe Collet, market gardener of Angers, a few days later. "It's scandalous," remarked a sewer digger in a small town in the south. Said a Parisian lady scornfully: "France is once more going downhill with a napkin under its chin."

After traveling through France for weeks, collecting these and similar opinions, talking to all sorts of people, . . . I understood the verdict of Deputy Paul Reynaud:

"France is the sick man of Europe."

[4] From "France Needs a New Revolution," by Edgar Ansel Mowrer, writer and commentator on world affairs. *Collier's*. 133:19-23. January 22, 1954. Reprinted by permission.

What's more, France's sickness seems unlikely to be cured by anything short of another revolution. I have come to believe we may see that revolution—a revolution with a small "r," to be sure, with no bloodshed, no reliance on a single strong man, nothing the Communists can seize upon and use . . . but a revolution nonetheless.

Short of revolution, the French seem condemned to play a less and less important part in today's world. Certainly they cannot continue to mooch along and duck essential issues in the weak hope that all problems will somehow solve themselves.

Nor can France hope to pull in its horns and take itself out of history. The nation is too big—larger than Great Britain and West Germany together—and too centrally located. France's neighbors simply cannot ignore France nor pass it by in their strategical calculations.

The French, now as in the past, seem destined either to remain co-makers of history or to lapse into subjugation or absorption by some less apathetic people. Which of the two extreme courses it will follow depends on whether the French can put an end to their recurrent governmental crises and establish real political stability. . . .

"All I know about French politics," a friend said to me in America, "is that every time the government has an important decision to make, it falls. Why?"

It falls because the governments of France must operate under a constitution which virtually guarantees weakness in office, which places the French executive at the mercy of an irresponsible Assembly, which provides for an advisory Council of the Republic instead of a Senate with real authority, which keeps the people from choosing their leaders or exercising any real influence over them.

Not everyone in France believes the 1946 constitution should be changed. But I found a powerful undercurrent of opinion, cutting across all groups, which favors a fresh start—a revolution—and the sooner the better. "Make France a modern nation." That's a slogan I heard from at least twenty of the hundred or more individuals I interviewed at length. . . .

How a nation runs its own affairs is, normally, its own business. But under today's critical circumstances, anything that weakens a portion of the free world becomes the business of free men everywhere. Frenchmen who feel at liberty to complain about American politics and economic policies should not object if Americans openly express the hope that France will put through needed reforms before it is too late. . . .

Yet before any thoughtful American decides to write France off he had better take a long look at what the French have accomplished since the end of a devastating war. Here is a list given me by one American diplomat who believes in France:

They have rebuilt all their bombed-out bridges, and more than half their war-damaged buildings. They have made their restored railroads the best in Europe. Six times as many tractors plow the rich farmlands. They have greatly increased industrial output, particularly of electricity. Certain industries and public works rival the finest in the United States. Their coal production per man has increased faster than any other West European country's.

They have raised the living standard to the prewar level —using only 66 per cent of their gross product as against 82 per cent in the thirties. Today, roughly 14 per cent of income is being reinvested, as against 3 per cent then.

The French have installed a social security and child-subsidy scheme at a cost of $1.2 billion annually, thanks to which the national health has been vastly improved and the population is increasing about 300,000 a year.

They are spending on national defense 50 per cent more, proportionate to income, than in 1938. They have stood the strain of a nine-year war in Indo-China that has cost them twice the amount of the United States aid received under the Marshall Plan.

Finally, . . . French minds have brought forth the most constructive ideas of the postwar West. One of these was the Schuman-Monnet Plan for the six-power coal and steel pool—since realized. The other was the Pleven Plan for combining the armed forces of the six into a single Army of Europe."

These are achievements to be proud of. Yet the terrible fact is, they are simply not nough. To see why not, a discontented member of the French Assembly suggested that I ask myself the following questions:

1. Does the French community provide as well as other comparable countries for the prosperity of its people?

2. Have the people enough confidence in their future to make an all-out productive effort and to take essential political, social and economic risks?

3. Are the people united enough to carry out positive policies both at home and abroad?

The answers, based on the best available information, are not encouraging:

1. According to French government statistics, taking the 1929 peak year as 100, today's French industrial production is still only 103. In Italy and West Germany, also war-ravaged countries, it is 144 and 125 respectively (using 1938 as the peak for Germany).

France is the finest piece of farm-land in Europe. Yet taking the average agricultural output of 1934-1938 as 100, France is now producing 103, while Britain,

Turkey, Switzerland, the Netherlands and Denmark are all reaching 120.

In both industry and agriculture, inefficiency shelters behind a wall of governmental protection. Although half of France's war-wrecked houses remain to be rebuilt, the present rate of moderate- and low-priced house construction falls below normal replacement in time of peace. It can hardly be increased so long as the government controls rents, the price of building material remains so high, and the French workers insist on such feather-bedding practices as first building walls and then tearing them down to insert pipes, meanwhile keeping Italian building companies, perhaps the world's finest, out of France by law. Millions of poorer people inhabit dwellings without sanitation, light or even fresh air, and young couples must double up with their parents.

The state subsidizes a long list of farm and industrial services and products. Despite such price supports and tariff protection, today the farmers are profoundly dissatisfied.

Moreover, lacking adequate capital, the French have partly financed their postwar activity by nourishing the cancer of inflation. As a result, in a country where perhaps a quarter of the individuals earn not over $100 a month, French prices are as much as 15 per cent above world prices. Sixty per cent of the state revenue comes from taxes on consumption. The value of the franc has fallen considerably—and there's no end in sight.

This, my rebellious young friends insist, is reconstruction at the expense of the widows, orphans, pensioners, insurance-policy holders—those on fixed incomes. The French people find themselves saddled with a system of huge private profits and socialized losses. Poorer people deliberately spend all they make.

France decidedly is not providing for its people as well as other comparable countries.

2. The French people have little confidence in their future, are not doing their best and are taking as few economic and political risks as possible.

Again the cause is partly economic. The rich sneak abroad what profits they can—where tax collectors and (perhaps) Communists cannot reach them. The smaller savers buy gold, which inflation cannot touch. Taken together, these estimated $4 billion to $6 billion of idle capital could vastly speed up French production, whose inadequacy is the main cause of France's woes.

The middle-of-the-road editor of *Le Monde,* Hubert Beuve-Méry, considers France's present decadence to be almost entirely the result of the timid, selfish, corrupt interests which perpetuate a system of high profits, limited output and limited risks.

Industrial and trade understandings (whose existence the participants blandly deny) serve to keep prices—and profits—high enough to protect the least efficient producers.

Trade is cluttered with speculators and middlemen ferociously indifferent to the effect on the consumer of their several takes. An outraged housewife near Chartres indignantly told me that one lot of vegetables was traced through twenty-six different hands between grower and consumer.

The workers reply by organized loafing—which, compounded by poor machinery and general inefficiency cuts heavily into production. On an average, the identical number of industrial workers who produce 100 units in France produce 180 in Great Britain and 310 in the United States.

3. The French people have been radically disunited since the original French Revolution in 1789. They

have—during my lifetime, at least—been a nation of grumblers. Yet today's disunity and discontent far exceed anything previously recorded. It's a discord that makes, say, the American quarrel over the New Deal seem insignificant.

But the ideological cleavage is as nothing compared to the economic discontent. As I wandered around France, questioning Henri, Jean and François, I could not escape one conclusion: the poor hate the rich, the workers and lesser employees hate the farmers, and the rich fear the poor.

Each can be justified.

The poor suffer from a pitiless price-wage scissors that the rich do their best to maintain. The rich have successfully blocked more equitable income distribution and stubbornly refuse to accept any larger share of the tax burden—or to pay honestly what they owe. Of the people who earned more than 3 million francs—$8,600— in 1952 (it's impossible to estimate their number, but it's certainly in the hundreds of thousands), only 28,800 declared that much income. When the Laniel cabinet started after the delinquents, it turned up people who owned villas, hired servants, drove cars—but insisted they had little or no income.

As for the peasants, they are believed to earn a quarter or more of the whole national income, but they manage to avoid paying any tax on most of it. In 1952, they paid 18 billion francs of income tax. Under a truly proportional charge, they would have paid more than 450 billion. The French often insist that Frenchmen pay "proportionately higher taxes than Americans." The obvious rejoinder is: "Which Frenchmen?"

The French budget has been continuously unbalanced, France is in debt about $1 billion to the European Payments Union (the clearing house for international trade payments), the franc is unstable, private investment remains small, France's great African holdings are only slightly developed. The greatly increased national production of which the country is capable fails to appear. . . .

Such a situation encourages dishonesty; bad morals inevitably follow bad morale. Until the French people see some worthwhile future they will continue to take the easy outs. And where can they discern any such future?

[Twelve] years after liberation, the French government has been unable to solve many of its vital problems, internal and external. Successive cabinets fear to tell the country the hard truth: France cannot afford to support farm products at prices which people cannot afford to pay. France must modernize its backward industries—or let them go broke. . . .

The French people cannot simultaneously agree to cooperate with West Germany, and refuse to cooperate; cannot want a united West Europe, and repudiate it; cannot rely for defense indefinitely upon the United States, and resent that reliance; cannot safely go on treating domestic Communists as though they were at the same time patriotic Frenchmen and partisans of a conquering foreign power.

Where in such a situation does a happier future loom? Is it any wonder that the average Frenchman, living without fixed purpose, seems instinctively to be expecting a new catastrophe?

THE FRENCH CRISIS IS ALSO MORAL [5]

Many Frenchmen—and most foreigners—look for the root of France's trouble in her political instability.

[5] From "What's Wrong with France?" by Guy de Carmoy, Inspecteur des Finances in the French Civil Service and lecturer at the Institut d'Etudes Politiques of the University of Paris. *Reader's Digest.* 64:117-22. May 1954. Reprinted by permission.

There is some basis for this: France's political feuds and weakness have undoubtedly hampered her industrial development. Yet this instability is not new. Since the birth of the French Republic in 1871 no premier has remained in office as long as three years. Only 10 have stayed for two years or more; 107 have not lasted a year.

This, however, did not prevent France from building the world's second-largest colonial empire, or from becoming one of the world's most prosperous nations. In the light of France's prewar record, political instability alone could hardly account for her present plight. . . .

In great part the French crisis is moral. Too many Frenchmen have developed the habit of seeking government protection. Industrialists, already protected against domestic competition by cartels, want the government to shield them against foreign competition by high tariffs and restrictive quotas. The peasants want government subsidies to enable them to buy the highly priced French manufactured goods. The workers want the government to supplement their inadequate wages with generous family allowances and other social benefits, while demanding at the same time the closing of borders to foreign labor, even when it is needed for expansion of the French economy.

No wonder, then, that 35 per cent of France's national budget goes for subsidies, direct and indirect, to business, industry and agriculture.

The French believe that they still have a free economy. What they actually have, in place of traditional free-market competition, is the competition for subsidies of innumerable groups, each of which presses the state to protect its acquired position by artificial means. Pulled in all directions by these competing pressure groups (each using one or two splinter parties to promote its interests), the government is no longer in a position to make the national interest paramount.

The price the French pay for this over-all protectionism comes high. For the government, unable to shoulder the heavy financial burden loaded upon it, has been compelled from time to time to lighten its burden by devaluing the French currency. . . .

A man who in 1928 placed his savings in French thirty-year bonds with the expectation of receiving a yearly income equivalent to about $6000 has in recent years been receiving the equivalent of only $315. And if he subscribed to $1000 worth of bonds in 1944, the value of his capital would by 1950 have decreased to $180.

Is it any wonder that the French have lost confidence in their currency? Many have even lost the traditional habit of saving. And of those who still do save, many look to gold as their best protection. The amount of French capital now being hoarded in gold has been unofficially estimated at $2 to $6 billion—several times greater than the gold reserve of the Bank of France!

France has also been suffering from uneconomic and inequitable tax laws. One often hears it said that the French do not pay taxes. This is not true; they are among the most heavily taxed people in the world. Their taxes amount to about 33 per cent of the gross national product, as against 27 per cent in the United States.

But nearly half the French budget comes from *sales* taxes. In contrast to his foreign competitor, the French industrialist must pay a high sales tax on all purchases designed to modernize his equipment. Then come sales taxes on the raw materials required for production. To these are added numerous sales taxes paid by the middlemen who distribute the product. All these taxes are passed on to the consumer. As a result commerce stagnates, the cost of living soars and the tax burden is borne primarily by those who can least afford it.

The French income tax, which contributes only about 30 per cent of the government's revenue, is a further example of an antiquated and unjust tax system. Peasants constitute more than a third of the population and earn about 15 per cent of the national income. Yet, because of privileges they receive under the law, they pay less than 3 per cent of the total income tax. Wage earners, who account for about half of the national income, pay 70 per cent of the income tax. It is inequity of this sort that has swelled the ranks of the dissatisfied.

Much has been made of tax evasion in France. It is certainly not as frowned upon among my people as it is in the English-speaking countries. But French treasury officials believe that loss of revenue from tax evasion is only half as great as from the disproportionate privileges established by the taxation system.

The damaging effect of inflation and uneconomic taxation in France is reinforced by two political factors: fear of war and fear of Communist influence at home. Added to this is the confusion resulting from the rather contradictory economic systems with which the short-lived governments experiment. The result: private capital investment for new means of production has almost ceased to flow.

In whatever direction we turn—peasants, workers, industrialists, tradesmen—few are willing to take a risk. Everyone is thinking in terms of security. And everyone wants his security protected by the state. This obsession gives the French economy an increasingly static character, which is, unfortunately, in line with the traditional French distrust of change. . . .

But much as we dislike it, the time has come for us to realize that unless we shortly make some drastic changes in our life and work we cannot continue to play a major role in world affairs.

To begin with, France must achieve a minimum of political stability. Because of the traditional fear of a strong executive, the 1946 constitution went too far in vesting so much political power in parliament. In 1953 the government undertook revision of the constitution; this program should be completed. The parliament must be made responsible for its action when it forces a government to resign. In England the defeat of a government on a matter of importance almost inevitably calls for new elections. In West Germany the Chancellor can be voted out of office only if the parliament agrees beforehand on his successor. It is unfair and inefficient that the French parliament should vote cabinets out of office without responsibility for the consequences.

A stable currency is at least as important as a stable government. Only if confidence in the currency is restored will it be possible to undertake the indispensable modernization of France's antiquated industrial and agricultural equipment.

The most urgent task ahead is the modernization of French agriculture. An American farmer produces food for 19 fellow citizens, a French farmer for only 6. In France there is 1 agricultural school for every 57,000 farmers, as against 1 for every 3300 farmers in Germany; France has 1 agricultural adviser for every 6000 farmers, as against Holland's one for every 240.

Agricultural experts have estimated that with the proper methods France could feed 70 million people—27 million more than her present population. Yet at present she is importing cereals, sugar, fruits, vegetables, eggs and dairy products at heavy expense.

Protectionist devices which make the French economy rigid and production costs high must be abolished. France is badly in need of anti-cartel legislation. And she must reconsider the aid now given to producers and exporters. Free competition, not subsidy, is the way to economic health. It is impossible, for example, for the government to go on buying alcohol from French distillers at four times the world price and selling most of it at a 75 per cent loss!

It is time to recognize that it was rigid rent control that blocked the construction of new houses. Most housing now being built takes the form of cooperative apartments—not subject to rent control—at prices only the rich can afford.

The tax system must be reformed so as to spread the burden more fairly and create incentive for productive investment. Nationalized industries must operate on balanced budgets. And the present controls on French imports must be lifted: if France wants other nations to buy her products she will have to buy theirs.

Unfortunately, the drastic reforms needed in the French economic system are not in the making. Nor is it likely that they will be made until France determines the role she wants to play in the construction of a new Europe, a Europe offering greater economic opportunity and military security. . . .

A common market for heavy industry is only the first stage in a program which should gradually embrace the other sectors of Europe's economy, as well as a common defense and a common political authority. . . .

In the present plight of the French economy, German competition would certainly be damaging. Someone has wittily remarked that French-German integration—the base for European integration—would be much easier if the Germans would get up an hour later and take an hour more for lunch. Yet France has no reason to lack confidence. If her agricultural production is lower per acre than Germany's, it is greater in volume. Germany is richer in coal, but France is richer in water power, iron ore and bauxite. And if France adds to her domestic potential the industrial, mineral and agricultural resources of her overseas possessions, there is no reason why she should fear German competition. What the French need to do is to get up an hour earlier and take an hour less for lunch!

If France and Germany maintain their present status as sovereign states, the chances are that Germany will continue her dynamic expansion while France slides further downhill. But if the two nations integrate their economies, France will find herself compelled to make the reforms indispensable to her recovery.

No great reform has ever been accomplished without faith. In their present national framework the French cannot find the necessary faith. But in the larger framework of a European community they are bound to find both the faith and the incentive to carry on the civilizing mission which has been theirs for centuries in Europe and in the world.

THREE NEEDS FOR REFORM [6]

The problem of making democracy work in France is by no means a new one. It would be hard to find a time during the past century when Frenchmen were generally satisfied with their governmental system and when various discontented groups were not trying to alter or replace that system. . . .

[6] From "Constitutional Reform in France," by Gordon Wright, professor of history, University of Oregon. *Foreign Policy Bulletin.* 32:58. June 1, 1953. Reprinted by permission.

French reformers, in their effort to improve the governmental machinery, propose a triple set of changes: in the electoral law, in parliament's rules of conduct, and in the constitution itself.

The electoral system which postwar France has used is a modified version of proportional representation. Its effect has been to perpetuate a multiparty system, with six parties about equally balanced in the National Assembly. It has also made the parties more rigid and disciplined than was the case in the Third Republic, for deputies have come to be more dependent on the party for renomination at each general election.

In theory, this increased rigidity of parties ought to make governmental coalitions more stable. In practice, such has not been the case. The principal effect seems to be that cabinet coalitions are now harder to form than they used to be. Another consequence of the proportional system is that it has protected the large minority parties. . . .

Some critics of this electoral system see it as the basic flaw in France's governmental structure, far more important than any constitutional weaknesses. They argue that the real barrier to efficient cabinet government is the multiparty system and that the task of achieving a stable majority can be accomplished only if something approaching a two-party structure emerges. They propose therefore, the adoption of an electoral system not used in France for more than a century. Its two key provisions would be (1) large multi-member electoral districts, with each party presenting a list of candidates equal to the number of seats, and (2) election by mere plurality of the leading party's entire list. This system, its sponsors contend, would put such a premium on electoral coalitions that soon only two or three major groups would remain. Then these coalitions, instead of disintegrating after election day (as is now the case), would probably develop into complete mergers within a few years. Real majority government by a single party might at last become possible in France.

There is much to be said for this scheme, but none of the Center parties is prepared to risk the possible danger that it might redound to the benefit of the Communists in those parts of France which are strongly Leftist and anticlerical by tradition, or to the reactivated Gaullists. . . .

A second category of reforms which is considered necessary by many Frenchmen concerns the internal functioning of parliament. The National Assembly makes its own rules and can alter them without need for constitutional revision. Critics have pointed out for decades that the legislative process in France is clumsy and inefficient and that the effect is to destroy popular confidence in democratic methods. These reformers urge, therefore, that the Assembly stop trying to legislate in detail on everything from Army appropriations to the number of stallions on the national stud-farms. They would have the Assembly reduce its inhuman burden by various devices, such as adopting general *lois-cadres,* or "framework-laws," which might be filled in by administrative action. The reformers also contend that the Assembly's system of specialized standing committees, which in their opinion impedes a vigorous governmental program, ought to be revamped or abolished. Reform of the Assembly's habits and procedures, however, will not come easily. Despite the critics, the legislators are intensely jealous of their prerogatives, and it seems unlikely that any major improvements will occur soon.

There remains the question of the constitution itself. That document has never won the respect or the affection of Frenchmen. When it was ratified in 1946, only 9 million citizens gave it their support, while 16 million voted against or stayed away from the polls. Revisionism was in the air from the very beginning; and pressure for change has increased by fits and starts since then. In November 1950 parliament adopted a resolution initiating the amendment of eleven specified articles of the constitution. An Assembly committee at once undertook to draft new versions of those articles, but two years passed and the task was still unfinished. . . .

But the problem of revision is not so simple as all that. One reason for the failure of the reformers to push through a single amendment since 1946 is the complexity of the amending process itself. The constitution's authors sought to guard against hasty changes by requiring (Article 90) a popular referendum unless parliament adopts an amendment by a large majority (two thirds of the lower house or three fifths in both houses). The Socialists and Communists, who oppose any fundamental amendments, have so far been strong enough to make either of these procedures risky. Some Frenchmen hold, therefore, that top priority should be given to an all-out effort to amend Article 90 in order to simplify the amending process. Efforts are also being made to secure a judicial reinterpretation of Article 90 so that a three-fifths majority of those deputies and senators *present* and *voting* (rather than of the total membership) would be sufficient.

There is, however, a much more important reason why the revisionists have not yet attained real results. After all, the revisionist parties probably have a clear majority in the country and, since the 1951 elections, a three-fifths margin in the two houses of parliament. If united, therefore, they should be able to proceed under Article 90 as it stands. But they are not united. Although most of them concur on certain issues, there are wide enough differences on several important points to make agreement difficult.

In general, the revisionists fall into three categories. The first group, which was also the most extreme and intransigent, was the Gaullist RPF (Ralliement du Peuple Français). The Gaullists have insisted ever since 1946 that the whole spirit and structure of the regime must be changed. They stress especially the need for a powerful executive, with the right to dissolve the National Assembly at will and with authority to appeal to the people by referendum in cases of legislative-executive conflict. The Gaullists propose to grant this authority, not to the premier, but to the president of the republic. Their program appears to call for the transmutation of the latter into a quasi-American-type president and of the premier into a quasi-British-type prime minister. The relationship between them remains one of the major uncertainties of the Gaullist blueprint. The RPF has also favored an increase in the powers of the upper house, the Council of the Republic, and its conversion into a semicorporative body.

The Gaullist program goes far beyond the wishes of the second major revisionist group, the centrist and rightist parties (Radical Socialists, Independent Republicans, and Peasants). These elements look back nostalgically at the prewar era and seek to make the Fourth Republic as much like the Third as possible. Their primary emphasis is upon a return to true bicameralism by restoring to the Council of the Republic most of the powers of the old Senate. The upper house has long been the special preserve of the Right-Center groups, since it is chosen by a special electoral system which gives great weight to the votes of the small-town and rural populations. They contend that this change would restore "balance" to the parliamentary system and that it would check hasty, demagogic action by the lower house. The Right-Center parties also propose to strengthen the executive somewhat by restoring two of the cabinet's prewar privileges: the power to dissolve the Assembly and the right to issue decrees with the force of law, when so authorized by the Assembly. It has been easy for the Gaullists to point out that neither of these prerogatives produced effective government before 1940.

The third major revisionist element, the Christian Democratic MRP (Mouvement Républicain Populaire) takes a more restrained approach. Its leaders were among the principal authors of the 1946 constitution; it therefore seeks to correct and improve that constitution, not to amend it out of existence. MRP spokesmen favor a number of more or less minor changes to correct technical flaws in the functioning of the system. More important, however, is their advocacy of the dissolution power for the premier. They vainly proposed the freer use of that power while the constitution was being drafted in 1946 but were then forced to compromise because of Socialist and Communist opposition. They now point out that dissolution in its present restricted form (Article 51) is totally inoperative; and they contend that there can be no stable and effective government until the premier can use the threat of dissolution to keep the Assembly in line.

Although these three programs overlap one another, the differences of approach have been enough to prevent any vigorous unified drive for reform. . . .

"What is needed," suggests *The Economist*, "is not a method whereby weak governments can be prolonged in office or given powers to legislate by decree, but a means of creating strong governments." One may legitimately doubt whether any program except that of the Gaullists could fulfill that need. But the Gaullist program offers little real hope to the friends of French democracy. For one thing, it contains too many potential booby-traps, such as the relationship between president and premier. Worse still, it arouses too many traditional doubts and suspicions on the part of the non-Communist Left and serves to divide Frenchmen rather than to bring them together. . . .

France needs change—political, economic and psychological change. On that fundamental point most Frenchmen and foreigners will agree. What is often overlooked is the fact that changes are occurring in France, just as in every other Western country. The process is perhaps much too slow for an age of crisis; yet it is more rapid than many people suppose. In the long run these evolutionary—almost geological—changes are more likely to preserve French democracy than any amount of constitution-tinkering. They portend a modified social and economic structure, a new type of industrial, technical and agricultural leadership, and perhaps a more widely diffused sense of civic responsibility.

Until this evolution produces measurable results, however, a heavy burden of responsibility must rest on the present leaders of France. Their primary task is to reconcile the conflicts among the various center parties, for, as Maurice Duverger points out, "without this reconciliation no real governmental stability can be assured, whatever may be the constitutional reforms." At the same time the Center leaders must somehow hold the support of the bulk of Frenchmen without falling back upon demagogic appeals to the special interests of their respective voting groups.

END OF A MINISTRY OF HOPE [7]

It was 5 A.M. in Paris [February 5, 1955]. A short, stocky man in a black topcoat hurried out of the old grey stone National Assembly building on the Quai d'Orsay. Minutes earlier Pierre Mendès-France had been Premier of France, the most popular, brilliant and energetic man to hold the office since the inception of the Fourth Republic. Now, ringing in his ears were the hoarse shouts and curses of his colleagues in the Chamber of Deputies still panting from the bitterest, most vindictive and unseemly overthrow of any premier in recent French history.

Job-hungry French politicians have a word, *usé* (used-up, soiled), for a government at the moment that it may be voted down and cabinet portfolios redistributed. . . . The opposition, having tried out its voting strength on a couple of small issues, and satisfied itself that Mendès was about *usé,* was ready for the big kill. Hunting ground : the debate on North Africa.

The dramatic moment came when ex-Premier René Mayer, an influential industrialist (identified with the Rothschild interests) and a member of Mendès' own Radical Socialist Party, took the rostrum. Mayer, whose constituency is Constantine in Algeria, was against Mendès' attempts to negotiate a North African settlement with the nationalist rebels. He was plainly on the side of the French settlers, and brushed aside talk of cruelty on the part of the French forces. "Repression always has a cruel aspect," he said coolly. "But this time it has been just. It was indispensable in order that the guilty might be punished. . . . It is essential that the Moslems faithful

[7] From "233 Days of Mendès-France." *Time.* 65:24-25. February 14, 1955. Reprinted by permission from *Time* Magazine. Copyright Time Inc. 1955.

to France, who have often been the victims of assassins, be effectively protected."

As Mayer spoke on, his voice rose, and the Assembly sensed that the "moment of truth" was at hand. "It has been said that France must adapt herself to the evolution of the modern world. If that means adapt herself as she has done in Viet Nam, or as she has done in the Fezzan and in the French establishments in India, I answer *non!*"

On the front bench, Mendès sat immobile, a little paler than usual, white cuffs peeping out from the sleeves of his dark suit. Mayer turned towards Mendès: "You have already asked many times for the confidence of the Assembly. Today personally I will not be able to vote for it. For I do not know where you are going." Gaullists, Catholic MRP's [Christian Democrats of the Mouvement Républicain Populaire] and Radical Socialists thundered applause.

Mendès spent the dinner hour furiously revising his speech of rebuttal. By 9 P.M. he was back in his seat. One by one the deputies drifted in. Dapper ex-Foreign Minister Georges Bidault, sniffing revenge (Mendès replaced him during the Geneva Conference), set down his briefcase, happily opened a newspaper. He was followed by seventy-six-year-old Paul Reynaud, who sat in the fifth row, his old hooded eyes staring straight in front and his head nodding constantly with a nervous tic. The galleries were jammed with spectators, among them Mendès' pretty wife. Outside stretched a long line of people hoping to be admitted to the few public seats.

Mendès walked briskly to the rostrum, opened a pink cardboard folder containing his speech, and began to speak quietly.

M. René Mayer has spoken of our errors and of their catastrophic results, of our heavy responsibilities. He has shared them and he still shares them, for he has supported with all his votes what we have done. If tomorrow the Assembly condemns us and blames us, it will also condemn and blame M. Mayer who has discovered six months late that the government has betrayed the country, liquidated French Africa and is unworthy of the confidence of the Frenchmen in North Africa.

For an hour and five minutes Mendès gave sturdy defense of his North African policy, enduring a score of interruptions, half applause, half boos and catcalls.

In a few biting phrases Mendès reproached the MRP for seeking vengeance for vengeance's sake:

There are only two possible policies in North Africa: that of cooperation and reforms or a policy of repression and force. The government has chosen the first. A fraction of the opposition is favorable to the second. Not all the opposition. The MRP will vote against because it wants to overthrow the government. So politics, odious politics, has once more altered the course of a grand debate on the fate of the nation.

Shortly before midnight he put the question of confidence.

A period of twenty-four hours must elapse between the posing and the taking of a vote of confidence. In this period the MRP caucus decided massively against Mendès. The Radical Socialists held a long, painful meeting in which Mendès and Mayer clashed. The party's Grand Old Man, Edouard Herriot (who had himself quarreled bitterly with Mendès over German rearmament), sent a message from Lyon asking the party to stick by Mendès.

At 2 A.M. the Premier mounted the rostrum. His hour was at hand. Precise and calm as ever, he placed notes in front of him, took a sip of milk, and immediately launched into a frontal attack on the MRP, which had charged him with "filling the prisons" in North Africa.

Though Mendès' rebuttal firmly placed the responsibility on the previous (MRP) government, his speech was grim confirmation of French colonial misrule. Said he:

In Morocco we found prisoners who had not even been convicted; among these prisoners, I scarcely dare report to the Assembly, was an eight-year-old child, who had been in prison for more than a year. In view of this, can anyone dare speak to this government of full prisons?

After a brisk, not altogether unfriendly series of exchanges with deputies, he concluded:

The debate this evening is not on changing premiers, but on making a choice in North Africa. I repeat this: the choice is among the gravest which the Assembly has had to make for many years. Perhaps the fate of France is at stake.

Ushers brought in the green urns, in which party leaders deposit either white cards (for the government) or blue cards (against). At 4:50 A.M., Assembly President Pierre Schneiter announced the official count: votes for the government, 273; against, 319—five more than a full majority. Said Schneiter: "Confidence has been refused to the Cabinet." But Mendès was not quite finished.

Taking the rostrum, he explained that he had not one word of recrimination against the Assembly decision. Deputies, accustomed to silence from defeated premiers, listened with astonishment as he went on:

The work accomplished by this defeated government will not be wiped out either in this field or in others. . . . What has been placed in motion will not be stopped.

Suddenly the pent-up tension of two days exploded in the Chamber. Deputies, outraged because they thought Mendès was appealing over their heads to the people, broke into an angry roar: "Fascist! Fascist!" They pounded on desks, booed, groaned, howled. Most noise came from the MRP. The Socialists (who had supported Mendès throughout) tried to drown them out with applause. MRP Deputy François de Menthon came running down the aisle, waving his arms, charging violation of parliamentary rules.

Mendès took a sip of milk, started to say, "The government has the right. . ." Louder and louder boos and the shrill screech of Communist women deputies in the upper register interrupted him. "The government has the right. . ." President Schneiter stood up, resplendent in white tie and tails, and called for order.

Mendès gripped the desk, leaned over, his face working with emotion, his lips phrasing sentences that only stenographers could hear:

. . . I know I have served my country well. I pray that in the future the Assembly may give Frenchmen new reasons for hope and may conquer the hatreds which it has too often put on display. *Vive la France!*

Now everyone was standing, booing or cheering. Mendès stepped down, picked up his briefcase, hurried out.

Behind him, as he climbed into his black Citroën, Pierre Mendès-France left not only a noisy Chamber but 233 days of accomplishment: He had:

Negotiated a cease-fire in Indo-China.

Forced the Assembly to decide on EDC [European Defense Community] (against) and then to accept German rearmament.

Opened negotiations for a settlement in Tunisia by offering autonomy.

Reached agreement with Germany on the Saar.

Persuaded Britain to keep four divisions permanently in Europe.

Restricted the overproduction of alcohol, issued free milk to schoolchildren.

Adopted several overdue constitutional reforms, introduced essential electoral reforms.

Raised the wages of industrial workers, and some government servants.

In his 233 days Premier Mendès-France had visited Geneva, Tunisia, Britain, Belgium, Canada, the United States, Italy and Germany, confronting chiefs of state as he conducted his own parliament, with subtly chosen, blunt decisions. He scorned the usual French political practices that exalted negativism into a philosophy. Watching him, millions of Frenchmen forgot their political lethargy and cynicism, cheered *"le style Mendès-France."* But the politicians whom he so coldly appraised as coldly disliked him. They feared his popularity and could not forgive him his success. They joined, Right and Left, to bring him down before he could proceed to the program he most wanted to put over: a dramatic overhaul of the French economic system.

The Assembly wanted no more energetic individualists for a while. President Coty's first choice for twenty-first premier of France since 1945 was Antoine Pinay, a small-time businessman with a reputation for getting along with people.

IN DEFENSE OF THE FRENCH [8]

There is a polite, cruel, old phrase in European diplomatic circles—"the policy of the empty chair." As you can imagine, it consists of treating a person—or a nation—as if he or it were not present, so his comments are not

[8] From article by Janet Flanner, Paris correspondent under the name of "Genêt" for the *New Yorker*. New York *Times Magazine*. p 12+. March 6, 1955. Reprinted by permission.

listened to and the nation's sovereign opinions are not consulted. Is this the kind of vacant seat, upholstered in the famous tricolor, that France has fixed for herself, and is going to be forced to occupy, because her allies think it easier to ignore her vagaries, her troubles and her presence?

A defense of France is not easy right now. Faith in her stability—other people's faith and, more important, her own people's faith—is at its lowest ebb since the war. The recent . . . period of confidence in France, which friendly nations and the French people, too, were pleased to have for a change, was exclusively synchronized with Pierre Mendès-France's dynamic regime . . . and was finished at the same moment he was voted out of power in Parliament . . . February 5 [1955]. . . .

In the outburst from the Paris press that followed his fall, three comments were particularly significant and seem worth citing even now. In a bitter editorial, *Le Monde* said in part, that afternoon:

Our allies across the Atlantic [meaning both England and the United States] would do well, before they start mourning for France, not to overwhelm France with their criticism. They themselves carry a large part of the responsibility for Mendès-France's failure. Their obstinacy in wanting to rearm Germany is without doubt the element . . . which finally provoked his fall.

The French historical memory is tenacious. It remembers the American Dawes plan and the Hoover moratorium, which, after the first war, helped put Germany back on its feet and save German investments for American banks; and it remembers England's aristocratic pro-German Cliveden set. Dean Acheson's 1951 plan to rearm Western Germany seemed to many French the same blind American diplomacy which after World War

I unconsciously helped Germany build up for World War II and was now rearming West Germans for World War III. And who could be sure, once Germany was in it, she would not help carve up France if only out of habit?

In a nutshell, it could be said that in killing EDC [European Defense Community], which Premier Mendès certainly did not try to save, a majority of France was speaking its mind in the vote of "no" on German rearmament, apparently to Washington's shocked surprise.

A few months later under Mendès' guidance, when the Chamber voted "yes" to his Paris Pacts' version of German rearmament—"You will have to vote it sooner or later," he calmly told the parliament, referring to semiofficial warnings from Washington that otherwise it would wash its hands of France—parliament was really voting "yes" to the Western Alliance, without which France would have stood alone. German rearmament was the thing Mendès paid double for. [For the action on EDC and the Paris Pacts, see the last three articles in Section II, below—Ed.]

First, it earned him the enmity of Georges Bidault's pro-EDC party, which, upon realizing the country's increasing anti-rearmament spirit, cleverly avoided ever proposing EDC to the vote, letting Mendès do it for them and take the failure and the blame and also their hatred. Then, when he put through the Paris Pacts, it cost him some antidisarmament chamber friends.

It could be argued by *Le Monde,* which never thinks highly of Washington diplomacy anyway, that Washington, with its insistence upon arming West Germany, was indeed partly responsible for Mendès' final fall—though a complexity of purely French angers and hopes, fears and interests were also involved, more subtle and more brutal than even French political incidents usually combine.

The second illuminating Paris newspaper comment after Mendès-France's overthrow—for it must be kept in mind as the most shaking personal political event in post-war France since the voluntary resignation from power of General Charles de Gaulle—was a melancholy *mea culpa* in *Le Figaro* next morning, saying in part:

Confidence in France is going through a crisis all over the world. There are doubts about what France wants, about what she says, about what she promises; there are doubts about what she really is.

After praising Mendès' energetic style as having left an unforgettable impression on the public mind, *Figaro* unfortunately went into prophecy, declaring, "The old merry-go-round of parliamentary ministers is no longer bearable and will not be borne" in selecting the incoming government.

Within two weeks the old parliamentary system of roundabouts, set rotating by opposing multiple political parties and their ambitious deputies, too often bent upon becoming ministers of anything whatever in an upcoming government, had whirled so dizzily that three designate-premiers in succession were prevented from making any government at all—MM. Pinay, Pflimlin and Pineau.

The third illuminating Paris newspaper comment came, the morning after Socialist Pineau's failure, from *Combat,* which said, "Everything shows that public opinion has speedily recovered its total indifference, based on contempt, to what systematically goes on now in the chamber."

So what next? What can the French people do considering this contempt for the selfish political power game that most of their elected national politicians play, careless of their country's good name or of what other countries think, indifferent to citizens' protests or newspapers' criticisms—a group of professional politicians mostly perfectly willing to let public opinion be dangerously divided or even to back a questionable party member, just to keep power intact? . . .

To bring in some new, younger blood as candidates for the coming elections, there may emerge an expanded political grouping, much talked about now, called *La Nouvelle Gauche,* the New Left. In January the art historian, André Malraux, who twenty years ago wrote the famous Chinese revolutionary novel, *Man's Hope,* and is now a leading Gaullist, said in part, in discussing the *Nouvelle Gauche* in an interview in the Mendèsist weekly, *L'Express*:

I think that a new phenomenon is taking place. Since the Liberation, on the whole, France has only conceived of the Right and Left in Marxist terms, with any French Left defined as proletariat and all the Right by its opposition to the proletariat.

But for more than a century France has been familiar with a Left defined by a state of mind, not by economics. It seems as if this Left is being reborn and as a singular, unexpected, new event, the renaissance of French liberalism. This liberalism is symbolized by Mendès-France . . . especially since France does not like its liberalism too soft. Mendès' energy is what sets his style.

The novelist and high churchman, François Mauriac, already leader of a new Left Christianism favoring social reforms for the empire's North African native population, which is still in a state of dangerous, unsettled crisis, is another noted literary figure in this new Left.

It is reported it might also have the backing of Claude Bourdet and his astringent intellectual political weekly, *France-Observateur,* plus that of the Catholic Church's most important liberal-wing periodicals, *Esprit* and *Témoignage Chrétien,* which, with *Le Monde* and, of course, *L'Express,* would try to organize this *Nouvelle Gauche* into cadres of voters as well as candidates for next year's elections, to bring Mendès to power as premier and hold him there until he had done a modernizing reform job on France's economy. If all this could be set going and really bear results, it could alter the face of France.

The French on both Right and Left consider it significant, naturally for different reasons, that Mendès, who had first named himself his own Minister of Foreign Affair to get Indo-China, the German question and the opening of the North African problem out of the way, had just named himself his own Minister of Finance so he could tackle economic reform—which is his special subject and his dominating interest in becoming Premier —when he was promptly overthrown.

Big business lobbies are as powerful in Paris as in Washington. Being a rich agricultural country that protected and was proud of its artisan class, France did not become industrialized in the last century as the island of England did, by necessity and through domination of a great foreign empire; or as the United States did, by settling, furnishing and developing its own vast territory and finding unexpected native wealth in raw material. The result of the French Revolution was to establish the French bourgeoisie in power, whatever people imagine to the contrary when they hear the music of the "Marseillaise."

And the bourgeoisie are always a cautious step slower than the working class or even the aristocrats. So it was that French business matured in an old-fashioned manner and behind the times because it was controlled by the

French bourgeoisie with their old habit and privilege of high profits, restricted production, high prices and small salaries.

Today the social security tax for family allowances puts a very heavy burden on the employer class since it supplements the increased wages employers rebelled against paying.

The fact that this family allocation money comes almost exclusively from the employer class' pockets makes the financial imbalance between the French boss and worker less extreme than some of France's critics realize. When there are French strikes, inevitably for more pay, it is naturally only the low wage figures that the strike leaders make speeches about that are most frequently reported in foreign newspapers.

A striker himself will loudly say, "I only earn 28,000 francs a month," without adding even *sotto voce*, "but in my case it adds up to 40,000 francs because my wife and I have a little boy and girl."

And, if he had three children, the family allocation would bring his income up to 49,000 francs plus a 30 per cent reduction on all rail and bus transport for the entire family. . . .

Since the war the French have increasingly realized that in order to compete with modernized countries in world markets France too must modernize. Rich Frenchmen who own factories tell you at cocktail parties that the retooling of France's industrial machinery is largely complete now and has at any rate more than made up for the five years it lost in the war.

The American system of what could be called participant capitalism, meaning that the workers' high wages give them a share of capitalism itself, is something the French capitalists have certainly never tried. Though the

American influence in general has constantly increased since the war, which may help restore some American confidence in France, it is very doubtful if the French will ever Americanize themselves to the extent of practicing planned obsolescence, which seems scandalous to their natural sense of thrift by which an object is used till it is worn out and not thrown out merely because it is last year's model.

Nor are they likely to take over the American system of buying everything on credit, so that if you pay cash for your American car or summer cottage, it looks as if you were naked of credit-rating and almost an unreliable citizen. It used to be considered estimable of the French that they like money, dislike paying it out but prefer to pay and be paid in cash, knowing it is cheapest in the end.

In any case, France's political instability does not affect her people's financial solidity, though saving money, under present high prices, has gone out of style.

The last time France had a severe financial panic was after the war of 1870, when it overstrained its reserves of wealth in paying off its war debt to Bismarck before it was even due. If one stops looking at the goings-on in the French parliament, France itself appears solid, a rich country by nature, with an ideal balance of about half its people on the land and the rest in industry, trade, commerce or the professions. . . .

A few years ago, after one of the twenty-one [plus] governments France has had since the war had fallen, there was an interval of almost a month in which there was no government at all. As if parliament were merely on a protracted holiday, the French people carried on in perfect shape, calm if grumbling and wounded in their pride.

The French Fourth Republic is certainly entitled to better and more stable government, and its citizens, just having lost the best chance of enjoying it that has come their way in a decade, will not be satisfied until France is more satisfactory.

As for the persistently worrying fact of French political instability that so agitates its allies, frankly the French are accustomed to it, as their last century's history shows. During the 1800's they tried once again every kind of government they had had before the Revolution and Napoleon invented one novelty in starting them off with a Consulate. Then came the Napoleonic empire, a Bourbon restoration which was an absolute monarchy, a small revolution, an ephemeral Second Republic, then another Bonaparte who began as President but was elected Emperor of a second Napoleonic empire, then a Paris Commune and finally the Third Republic.

The present Fourth Republic shows no sign of becoming anything else, but of continuing, as France has for 150 years, with political party confusions, which may grow less, and reliable prosperity.

THE NATURE OF FRENCH COMMUNISM [9]

The January 1956 Communist vote was almost the same as that in the national election of November 1946 when France was emerging from war and devastation, when she had not yet rebuilt her economy or stabilized her currency and was living on very short rations.

For many observers in France and abroad, these facts do not seem to make sense. They appear to indicate that the Communists do about as well at the polls in good

[9] From "The Red Vote in France," by Harold Callender, chief of the New York *Times* Paris bureau. New York *Times*. p3. January 9, 1956; and "The Paradox in France," by Harold Callender. New York *Times*. p3. January 10, 1956. Reprinted by permission.

times as in bad; that approximately one fourth of the French voters back Communist tickets whether the people are tightening or loosening their belts. It seems necessary to conclude that there is no clear correlation between Communist votes and the standard of living of the mass of the people.

In other words, the economic interpretation of history, a Marxian doctrine attributing all social phenomena to the economic condition of the peoples involved, does not seem to apply to the advance of the Communist party in Western Europe, or at least in France.

If this is a point against Communist dogma, it seems also a blow at the theory that a sure cure for the Communist infection is to raise the standards of living.

The figures of votes in France do not bear out this theory. In the grim year of privation, 1946, the Communists reached a high point by polling 5,475,955 votes, or 28.2 per cent of the total. In the far better but still uncertain economic conditions of June 1951, they polled 5,011,252 votes or 26.5 per cent of the total. In highly prosperous January 1956, they . . . polled 5,426,803, or 25.6 per cent of the total.

Thus at a time when France's production was about 70 per cent above that of 1938, and real wages had risen about 25 per cent in four years, the Communist vote was not far below its high point of the depressed year 1946.

This would indicate there was a kind of hard core of Communist votes that increased as the voting rolls increased and hovered with relative stability at about one fourth the total votes cast, regardless of economic conditions. This relative stability applies to French votes on the whole as divided among Left, Right and Center—a measure of stability at the voting level that insures instability in parliament because of the comparatively permanent divisions it creates there.

The members of the Communist party are fewer than half a million, or less than one tenth of the Communist voters. Thus at least nine tenths of those who vote Communist are non-Communists in the party sense. The bulk of these non-Communists who vote Communist are wage earners, but among them are also peasants, small tradesmen and even well-to-do farmers and intellectuals. Possibly not far from half the wage earners habitually vote Communist.

In the highly modern Michelin tire factories at Clermont-Ferrand, where wages far above the average are paid and many social amenities supplied almost free, the Communist-led unions of the General Confederation of Labor have long controlled the shop committees by virtue of the workers' votes.

When asked why this was so, a non-Communist labor leader said it was because the workers, although well paid, were treated about like machines if not rather worse. He said there were eighteen or twenty Communist cells in the factories, that the Communist secretary of these groups was also a Communist candidate in the national election.

The non-Communist labor man said the Communists successfully merged their trade union activity and their political activity, thus transferring to the party the allegiance won in the workshop on a strictly trade union basis.

He contended that the company, generous with its pay, neglected or opposed the unions; consequently, that the workers felt they were not treated with sufficient consideration and that they voted Communist to annoy the management.

The wage earner wants and fights for higher living standards. But there is no given point at which his aspirations stop and are replaced by complete contentment. Nor can these aspirations be measured exclusively in terms of purchasing power. The French worker is heir to a revolutionary tradition and is citizen of a republic upon whose official motto the word "equality"is inscribed as an apparent aim or promise.

He lives in a country that has long prided itself upon representing humanism in all its aspects. He has thus been taught to consider that every individual possesses certain inherent rights, which give him a kind of dignity that all must respect, however humble his social position.

This dignity may be as important to him as his pay envelope, or so he feels at times. Therefore the attitude of management toward him and his trade unions is almost as vital as the wages it grants. . . .

The French worker knows as little of . . . Communist totalitarianism as he knows of American capitalism, where mechanized production has produced the highest standards of living. In voting Communist, he does not vote for Moscow nor for Karl Marx' philosophy; he votes "to annoy the management," to express his dissatisfaction and perhaps his wounded dignity, and also to give what seems to be their due to labor organizations and leaders he believes work hard in his interests.

He also votes in favor of aims much like those of the Labor party in Britain, and he votes Communist because no other party and no Left group appears to him so effective an instrument. . . .

The Communist party profits from . . . [a] tradition which causes millions of Frenchmen to vote as far Left as possible. They consider the Communist party Left, although Guy Mollet, the Socialist leader and one of the most anti-Communist of Frenchmen, says the Communists are not Left but "East"—that is, tied to Moscow.

There is the story of a well-to-do farmer in the center of France who said he voted Communist because his father and grandfather had always voted Left and he did not intend to depart from this practice. Neither he nor the peasants who vote Communist are bothered by the fact that in the Soviet Union farms have been collectivized.

It is not long since the Communists were highly respectable in France. Soon after the Liberation, General Charles de Gaulle, heading a provisional government, brought the Communist leader, Maurice Thorez, back from Moscow and put him in the cabinet. Communists had joined with Catholics and others in the Underground while they were persecuted by Hitler and Marshal Pétain's wartime regime in France. So in 1944 and until about 1947 the motto of the moderate parties was "No anti-Communism."

Since the Communists have been isolated politically (from 1947), they have intensified their propaganda. In the recent campaign, they spent large sums on newspapers and leaflets distributed at factory doors. In the north, they held meetings for women at which were read letters from French soldiers in North Africa complaining of their lot.

The theory that higher living standards should cut the ground from under the Communists involves the same error as that of the economists a century ago who based their "economic laws" upon an "economic man" who existed only as a working hypothesis. Man is economic, but much else besides.

It is a paradox that the Communist movement, which both in Russia and France tramples under foot the rights and dignity of the individual, can nevertheless exploit the belief of many Frenchmen that their own state has sometimes been a bit careless of those rights and that dignity.

Much puzzled comment has been provoked by the fact that one fourth of the French voters cast ballots for Communists in the January 2 [1956] national election.

Some find it difficult to understand that this should take place after four years of rising wages and increasing prosperity. . . .

Some of the historical and psychological reasons for this apparent paradox were cited . . . [above]. There also are strictly economic reasons, notably the following:

Few wage earners give the government much credit for the rise in real wages resulting from expanding production. They are disposed to see them rather as gains won by trade unions. So they are more inclined to give the credit to the Communist-led General Confederation of Labor.

The economic advance of the last four years, which economists consider precarious, has not lasted long enough to make a great impression on the wage earners, who for a generation have habitually voted Communist.

Whether a continued expansion of the economy with a rise of real wages would cut down the Communist vote may be doubted in the light of recent history. It is noteworthy that the Communists are strongest among some of the highest paid workers, notably in the metal, printing and some building trades. So higher standards of living do not appear necessarily to turn workers away from Communist leadership.

The economic gains made while France has rebuilt her economy, partly with United States aid, have not yielded benefits so prompt or extensive to the wage

earner as to remove or greatly diminish his hostility to
what he calls capitalism.

In the latter days of the United States Economic
Cooperation Administration, which directed the Marshall
Plan in Europe, its officials were deeply concerned by
the absence of evidence that this huge and costly enter-
prise had had any effect on the mind of the French
wage earner. For he seemed as prone as ever to vote
Communist in the shop and at the ballot box. Much
United States propaganda was designed to enlighten the
French worker about United States capitalism, but there
is no sign it has cut into the Communist vote.

So far as this propaganda had any effect, it may have
added to the French worker's discontent by showing him
how low his wages were in comparison with those of
workers in the United States. Praise of capitalism in the
United States could hardly help appearing to be indirect
criticism of French capitalism.

There probably is no fully accurate way to measure
standards of living based on different currencies and
ways of life. The fact that a recent agreement fixed the
pay of the highest category of French coal miners at
the equivalent of 40 cents an hour probably would lead
to an underestimation of French real wages in comparison with those in the United States. But by any meas-
urement the French wage level in general is considerably
lower than that in the United States.

Statisticians here say the proportion of the national
income received by wage earners—about 30 per cent—
has not greatly varied in recent years. Wages have risen
with national income and not much faster. Thus the
worker seems at least to be holding his own.

But this result did not meet the worker's fullest
aspirations. One reason is that his standard of living
could not be measured by wages.

Though his wages had been doubled, he still could not have acquired much better housing, since it did not exist for him to rent or buy.

House building has lagged far behind in France. Recent figures show that in each year since 1951 the houses built fell far below the number promised by the government. In 1955, the number planned was 250,000, but the number built was 205,000.

A recent study indicated that in French towns with populations of more than 10,000 overcrowded dwellings housed 21 to 24 per cent of the people. Another study led to the conclusion that in towns with populations in excess of 30,000 only two thirds of the dwellings had electricity and water.

Bathrooms still are rare in wage earners' houses. This study found that in Paris they existed in only 17 per cent of the apartments.

As regards housing, the responsibility is mainly that of the government. Rents have been kept artificially low for a long time, hence private capital has gone into luxury dwellings only. Low rents helped the workers, but they also prevented his getting better housing until the government should provide it, which it is doing very slowly.

A wage earner whose pay rises but who must go on living in a slum hardly believes his standard of living has risen.

The conclusion confirmed by many expert observers here is that so far there is no visible relationship between rising wages or rising living standards and the votes the Communists poll in France. Some of the reasons for this are to be found in French history, the Communists having to some extent inherited the tradition of the Jacobins (the extremist club during the French Revolution).

But if it be assumed that raising the standard of living will cut down the Communist vote in the long run, there are fairly clear reasons why it has not begun to do so yet.

THE NEW FACE OF THE FRENCH RIGHT [10]

French democracy's senior ill-wisher, the Communist party, made its presence felt in the elections of January 2, winning a fourth of the nearly 22 million votes cast in metropolitan France and 145 of the metropolitan's 544 seats in the National Assembly. But this was to be expected. The Communist gain of more than fifty seats compared with 1951, when elections were last held, was due to the weird workings of an electoral law that had in effect counted out many of their 1951 ballots. . . .

What was not expected was the success of the Union de Défense des Commerçants et des Artisans, the personal creation of Pierre Poujade, the thirty-five-year-old self-styled Little Stationer of Saint Ceré (a village of 3,200 people in south central France). UDCA, running without any coherent program, won more than 2.5 million votes and fifty-two Assembly seats. . . .

Whatever short-run palliatives are applied, the long-run chances of French parliamentary democracy must be measured against the cold fact that in this highly literate country, in the midst of the greatest economic boom Europe has ever known, four voters in every ten voted for parties—Communist or Poujadist—that make no effort to mask the contempt in which they hold political democracy or of their desire to dismember it. The existence of the Communist threat, its causes and its

[10] From "Why the French Act That Way," by Harry L. Turtledove, author and authority on French affairs. *Harper's Magazine.* 212:71-6. May 1956. Reprinted by permission.

strength, are well known. But the newest menace has been little known outside France and not fully appreciated there. . . .

The consensus of the experts is that Poujadism is a movement of shopkeepers and artisans united in the interests of tax reform, and that its unexpected electoral showing resulted from its capture of the votes of the chronically disgruntled. Such capsule evaluations are convenient for newspapers, and true as far as they go. But they do not explain why a so-called tax-reform movement should win so much support at the expense of the established parties—which, after all, cannot be unaware of the need for tax reform—nor why there should be, at a time when French production and consumption are at all-time record levels, 2.5 million "disgruntled" Frenchmen in addition to the other 5 million who vote regularly for the Communists. . . .

To accept Poujadism as a tax-reform movement is to miss its real meaning. The Little Stationer of Saint Ceré has not suddenly become a major political force among the lower middle class because he has convinced them that they should no longer pay the taxes most of them were not paying in the first place. His movement has suddenly become powerful because it accurately reflects and exploits the nihilistic desire of millions of Frenchmen to reject the twentieth century—and with it a political system that has provided no solution to the real economic problems which they face. Hence Pierre Mendès-France's observation, the day after the elections, that the Poujadist surge was attributable to "ten years of *immobilisme.*"

France is really the nation of shopkeepers. . . .

The French *commerçant* occupies a position described in no orthodox economic textbook. Just as the

French manufacturer is spared external competition by all kinds of barriers, of which high tariffs are only one, so the merchant is relieved from internal competition by a highly cartelized industry and an all-interfering government that, combined, produce rigidly fixed retail prices. Spared from the most telling form of competition—price rivalry—the French merchant has become, for the most part, a glorified order-taker. He is often unqualified, generally under-capitalized, dependent for a living in an over-crowded trade on a small volume of sales. His prices—both those fixed for him and the few he fixes for himself—are consequently set high enough to yield a large profit on each sale. He is seldom equipped, either mentally or materially, to sell in volume, and the idea that he could better himself by selling more for less is alien.

To be sure, many small merchants have done, and still do, very well; their real profits are well-kept secrets, sometimes hidden—because of their distrust of accounting and distaste for candid bookkeeping—even from themselves. But one has only to visit the shops of a few French towns, with their plethora of dingy little groceries, bakeries, bars, and dry-goods stores to realize that many others live close to poverty. They do not go bankrupt only because their capital investment is hardly greater than their small inventories (they get little or no credit), they pay no wages (the family does the work), and the back or upstairs of the shop provides them with living quarters.

This is a general situation, but it is most acute in the south and west, those depressed areas that have lagged progressively farther behind as other areas have boomed, making the national maldistribution of capital, industry, talent, and imagination ever more lopsided. Much has been said about pouring new economic life into these regions; next to nothing has been done. Small wonder that it was below the Loire—roughly the northern border of the depressed areas—that Poujadism was born and flourished.

Here then is a living anachronism composed of thousands of people. Insecure in their declining social status but fearful that they will lose even what little remains, anxious for change yet aware that many of them could not survive any rationalization of the French economy, bitter because successive French governments have ignored the basic problem but fearful of what a courageous government might do, they solace themselves in escape. Escape to the days when life was "simpler," when there was, ostensibly, no Big Business or Big Government, when France basked in her glory, and a man could make his living in peace. Not Reform but Return is their goal.

To a class with this mentality, living in an atmosphere of general political irresponsibility whose tone was often set by the National Assembly, the Little Stationer of Saint Ceré was a natural leader. And his ideas grew with his popularity. From preaching tax "reform" to interfering with tax collectors, and then even to relieving them of their collections, was a short step. The big step was the one into politics.

The experts in Paris scorned Poujadism's political chances. The movement would fail, they said, because it had nothing to offer. But Poujade did have something to offer: a diagnosis and a cure for the ills of the times. The diagnosis was simple: throw all the corrupt (*i.e.,* the elected officials) out of office. So was the cure: the call for an Estates General.

What better scapegoat for France's ills than her institutions of popular government? What more ingenious exploitation of the desire to look backwards than to suggest a return all the way to the eighteenth century? Of course, Poujade never explained how that feudal institution, the Estates General—whose last session, in 1789, ended with its transformation into the original National Assembly—would accomplish what that new institution, universal suffrage, could not. Nor did he explain with any precision how his Estates General would be convoked, any more than he explained what his position was on Algeria, housing, wages, European defense, farm policy, governmental reform, or any of the other problems with which France is confronted. It was sufficient for him to reply—when, rarely, these problems were forced on his attention—that when the Estates General was called the "will of the French people" would be known. . . .

Poujadism is not fascism in the "classical" sense, for it lacks the philosophical mumbo-jumbo that gave fascism an ideology and an "idealism." But if fascism, with all its philosophy, culminated in nihilism, Poujadism goes it a step better by starting with nihilism.

At the moment, the movement probably owes a greater debt, unacknowledged though it may be, to that poisonous precursor of fascism, Maurras, than to Mussolini or Hitler. And if it possesses the general fascist characteristic of representing authoritarianism while at the same time attacking authority, it is also peculiarly French in holding out visions of the kind of anarchy ("order" in the midst of freedom from the responsibilities of citizenship) that is so cherished by the French bourgeois mind.

Like all fascist movements, Poujadism is a middle-class revolt motivated by fear. Yet, unlike his predecessors, Poujade has not made the working class and the fear of Communism—even in a country where Communism is a real and persistent threat—his main target. That position has been reserved for the democratic system generally—and particularly for Mendès-France and his political allies as the force most likely to reform the system. The tacit and cynical electoral truce between the Communists and Poujadistes spared each partner the attacks of the other, thereby allowing both to concentrate on their common enemies, the supporters of parliamentary democracy. . . .

Certain French observers have been at pains to demonstrate that the latest elections really show that not much has changed since 1951. Then, they point out, the extremists (Communists and Gaullists) polled about 9 million (45 per cent of the total) votes; this time, they polled roughly 8.5 million (40 per cent), the Poujadists having replaced the now scattered Gaullists. Ergo, there is a fairly constant proportion of malcontents among the French electorate.

Now there can be little doubt that many, though far from all, of Poujade's supporters voted Gaullist in 1951. But that in no way diminishes the vast difference between the two movements. Gaullism was built around the unquestionably outstanding French figure to emerge from the war. It was founded on a mordant analysis of the weaknesses built into the structure of the Fourth Republic—an analysis that has proved all too accurate—which was shared by noted Frenchmen in all walks of life, including intellectuals like Malraux and Mauriac. While Gaullism was unquestionably strongest among the middle class, it was not without a following among the working class; its left wing was made up of men with strong views who thought they saw in a French state with de Gaulle in command the only chance of obtaining fundamental social and economic reform.

Gaullism, of course, had its weaknesses. Two of them were fatal: the failure of its mystical leader ever to state precisely what he intended to do with the power he solicited, and the gradual taking over of the movement, through the workings of a sort of Gresham's law of French politics, by its worst elements—the discredited careerists, ultra-reactionaries, and, by supreme irony, the Vichyites and their camp followers. By 1951, when it made its supreme bid for power, Gaullism was already in decline and had lost many of its most distinguished followers. But even at that late date, men of high standing and integrity participated in the "Rally of the French People."

Poujadism is a solid one-class movement. No French notable in any walk of life is associated with it. It has no working-class following, and whatever support it receives from industrialists and big businessmen—most of whom undoubtedly prefer the "reasonable" Right personified by M. Pinay—is surreptitious. To travel from Gaullism to Poujadism in less than five years is to go a long way—all of it downhill.

It is all the more remarkable that this degeneration has taken place during the most prosperous years that France—though not necessarily all Frenchmen—has ever known and when, in the popular French view, the threat of war is less serious than it has been for a long time. If Poujadism is the product of peace and prosperity, what can be expected from bad times?

DE GAULLE IN RETROSPECT [11]

The only gigantic figure on France's mid-century scene has been that of the sad, embittered, arrogant and lonely Charles de Gaulle. Now living out a self-imposed

[11] From "The Age of Giants Is Over: III—France," by C. L. Sulzberger, New York *Times* correspondent. New York *Times.* p 14. August 4, 1956. Reprinted by permission.

retirement on a modest village estate, the haughty general has, like the aged Churchill, turned largely to a literary career. Each day he works with painstaking precision upon his memoirs, writing in pinched, labored hands, undeterred by weakening eyesight, unwilling to dictate because he feels this hampers proper compositional balance. The result is elegant French prose.

But de Gaulle's renown will not be based upon excellence of a memorial style. During World War II he salvaged his nation's self-respect. After the occupation, as head of Paris' Provisional Government, he reinstilled among his countrymen the concept of *grandeur*, of a great French global role.

This insistence upon national eminence was not recognized by the realities of an atomic age. In the Levant, in Indochina, in North Africa the overseas empire cracked off and vanished into the anticolonial tide. And metropolitan France herself, despite a rising birthrate and a balanced internal economy, never managed fully to recapture the full vigor of political or productive energies.

Many attribute to de Gaulle himself considerable responsibility for these failures which succeeded the romance of his Lorraine cross. Uncompromising, ill-adapted to harmonizing opposite views, the general showed scant political talent. Diplomatically his eye was fixed upon the lofty dream of a great imperial France. Therefore his slowly recovering country lost opportunities in statesmanship.

In 1946 King Haakon of Norway observed that all the Continental lands were seeking French leadership to unite them as a bloc between the two extra-European superpowers; but that de Gaulle blindly ignored this chance. He insisted on playing a global role that France's energies were unable to fulfill.

The general toyed with odd political formulas like that of labor-capital "associations" reminiscent of the outmoded corporate state. He awarded high governmental positions to Communists before deciding, all too late, that they must be banned from politics as Soviet collaborators. He squabbled with Right and Left, disdained advisers, irritated allies and infuriated many of his friends. Finally, in 1946, he resigned his office only to organize a strange non-party coalition, the RPF [People's Rally], which failed.

For the better part of a decade, as France skidded from one political crisis to another, the gloomy general has sat stolidly upon the sidelines confiding sardonic observations to his callers, predicting pitfalls and disasters. Yet, removed as he is from the active stage, the very existence of his vigorous personality reminds many Frenchmen of a possible alternative if chaos ever comes. That alternative would be de Gaulle, vested with true executive authority.

Since he departed, French politics has resumed its traditionally tragic game of musical chairs. The National Assembly, made up of remarkably intelligent individuals, has been paralyzed all too often by indecisions only resolved by agreement to topple governments. One party after another has sought to guide a coalition to durable success and failed. One astute politician after another has attempted to galvanize the nation and plan a long-range future. Yet none has for long impressed his views or personality upon his countrymen.

The French people simply refused to give sufficient constitutional authority to their premier. As de Gaulle had the acuity to foresee but not the ability to forestall, this led to paralytic tendencies and legislative chaos. Mollet, hard-working and courageous premier of the moment, has fought against this situation energetically. He succeeded astonishingly well in meeting grave crises with considerable success. But this is to a degree the result of a temporary political truce: no other party yet wishes to shoulder the burden of responsibility.

Effective government is difficult for long in France because of a deep-seated suspicion among its citizens of moves to develop the executive power. Experiences with dictatorship, headed by those of the two Napoleons, sometimes exaggerate French concepts of democracy to an anarchic point.

A feeling of impotence has crept across the national consciousness, succeeding brave, brief dreams of post-war grandeur. Capital has fled or been secreted. Productivity is hit by lassitude. Unfair taxation has induced the resentments expressed by the pitiful Poujadist movement. [See the preceding article, "The New Face of the French Right"—Ed.] Hurt feelings of nationalism inspire indifference with hints of xenophobia.

Only disaster in 1940 produced the solitary giant of this era in French history. And only when France was in her lowest depths was de Gaulle truly successful. Surely only another disaster could restore him to the active scene. Meanwhile our oldest ally, led by sincere and able men but of no towering stature, engages in successive battles for survival as a factor in the world.

II. FOREIGN POLICY

EDITOR'S INTRODUCTION

French foreign policy since the end of World War II has followed an erratic course. At times it has taken sudden, dramatic turns, as, for example, the French rejection of the European Defense Community (EDC) and the recent French intervention in Suez. One of the primary considerations affecting the direction of French policy throughout the postwar years has of course been the cold war. As it became warmer, in the late forties, the French were under increasing pressure to follow the United States lead in strengthening the ties and defenses of the West. More recently, after the death of Stalin and the subsequent letup in tension between East and West, the French began to see themselves in a more neutral role. By the summer of 1956, the pendulum had swung part-way back to middle ground between the United States and the U.S.S.R., and the French were ready to attempt a course of peaceful coexistence with the countries of Eastern Europe. The events in late 1956, the double impact of the Suez crisis and the Soviet subjugation of Hungary, however, at once put a severe strain on French-U.S.S.R. relations and forced the French back into the embrace of the United States and the Atlantic Alliance.

Considerations other than the cold war have also directed the course of French foreign relations in the postwar years. While France emerged from the war considerably weakened as a major power, she has nonetheless not adjusted easily to playing a secondary role in world affairs. Thus, under the de Gaulle government, she sought to regain prestige by acting as mediator between East and West. And later she attempted to secure a position of leadership in Western Europe by evolving the concept of West European Union. Then there is the age-old rivalry between France and Germany, which revived with Germany's rapid recovery from wartime defeat. Most observers believe it was fear of German resurgence that was behind the rejection of the proposed European Defense Community in 1954. Other guiding factors have been the continuing crisis in French internal politics and, as in the Suez situation, the constant ferment in the French overseas possessions, notably in Indo-China and North Africa.

In this section an attempt is made only to hit the high points, or low points, in French foreign relations in the last twelve years. The section deals mainly with the various proposals for uniting Europe—politically, militarily and economically. It does not cover the Suez crisis, because it was felt that the French position was closely allied with the French problem in North Africa. A discussion of the Israeli-French-British intervention in Suez and its ramifications is taken up in the following section on North Africa and the Suez crisis.

In the first article in this section, D. W. Brogan, an authority both on France and the United States, discusses the stresses and strains in the Western big-three alliance; although he was writing in the less tense atmosphere of 1954 his main conclusions still seem valid today. The next article provides general background information on the development of French foreign policy from 1945 to 1954. Robert Schuman, who has been Foreign Minister in successive postwar French cabinets, describes the concept and aims of the Coal-Steel Community, or the Schuman Plan, of which he was the author. A New

York *Times* article by Lansing Warren traces the history of the idea for the European Defense Community. An editorial published in the New York *Times* the day following the French vote on EDC gives a semi-official United States reaction to its defeat. Two opposing arguments on the French rejection of EDC are set forth by *Times* correspondent Herbert L. Matthews and Professor Saul K. Padover. A part of the text of the London and Paris Agreements, on freeing and rearming Germany, is included to round out the discussion of European defense; the Agreements (also called the "Paris Pacts") were negotiated as an alternative to EDC and ratified by the French Assembly on December 30, 1954. The section closes with two comments on the latest plan for European economic integration, which was prompted evidently by the political and economic impact of the Suez crisis.

HOW FIRM IS THE WESTERN ALLIANCE? [1]

When Foch was an instructor at the Ecole de Guerre before 1914, he was a devoted, almost uncritical admirer of Napoleon. Much later, he confessed that his admiration had been considerably modified, not because he had victoriously commanded a much bigger army than Napoleon ever did, but because as the Commander in Chief of a "coalition" army he had learned how much easier was the task of the leader of a unified, national force. Facing allies, Napoleon had half his problems solved for him.

What is true of hot war is true of cold and as Sir Winston Churchill makes plain in the last volume of his memoirs, even in hot war, the political cracks of the cold war were visible. Thus we might as well begin by ac-

[1] From "Can the Western Three Ride the Storm?" by D. W. Brogan, professor of political science, Cambridge University, Cambridge, England. New York *Times Magazine*. p9+. May 16, 1954. Reprinted by permission.

cepting the fact that all alliances make great claims on the wisdom, patience, loyalty and even humor of the high contracting parties and, what is more serious, of the peoples they represent. There is nothing, that is to say, odd, surprising, or in itself especially disturbing, in the fact that the three main allies in the NATO set-up—the United States, Britain and France—do not see eye to eye all the time, that the peoples of these three countries are not one happy family, that at moments (and this is one of them) the strains may seem to be so great as to threaten the very existence of the alliance. And the strains will certainly threaten the alliance if the basic causes of the strains are not allowed for.

There are occasional causes, special problems that affect one or more partners in such a way as to make unity difficult, crises that lead to public or private name-calling. But behind the high points on the fever chart lies the constitution of the patients.

First of all, it must be noted that two of the patients (if the medical metaphor is permitted) are not suffering from a mere fever; each is, in different ways, recovering at varying rates of speed from a very serious and de-bilitating illness. This, Britain and France have in common. The ordeal each underwent in the last war was different, but each nation is anemic, shocked, enfeebled by an experience that, at the very least, brought out the immense strength of the United States which now knows itself to be the most powerful nation in the world. . . .

Why is France the weakest spot in the North Atlantic armor? First of all because of certain intrinsic weaknesses that are indisputable. By every standard of comparison, France is much weaker than Britain and of course, far, far weaker than the United States. France, as the weakest ally, is thus subject to the most serious strain in keeping her end up. Her inferiority in population, capital equipment and all forms of wealth, plus her visibly exposed position on the Continent, make her situation difficult and the alliance especially burdensome (it is also especially valuable, but that is another story).

But France is weak and vulnerable in another way. The British decline is mainly relative. France's is probably absolute. In the two wars France suffered immense losses in life (even in the second war she lost more than Britain or the United States) and in wealth so that, by 1939, she had not recovered from the war of 1914-18, and in 1954 she has not recovered from the war of 1940-45.

This material loss is one factor to be borne in mind. Another, and one equally important, is the shock to the French psyche given by the two wars, by the intolerably costly victory of the first and by the disasters and humiliations of the second. If the French seem to many Americans unduly afraid of anything that can be made to seem to lead to war, the reasons are very human, very deserving of sympathy. No reproaches, no sermons, no brisk admonitions will wipe out the memory of Verdun or of the German Occupation. That, again, is a basic truth to be remembered.

But it is not merely a question of the French psyche as shocked by the two great wars of this century. Some of the French divisions and French weaknesses go back to the French Revolution. They are, if you like, nobody's fault, but there they are. *No* government in France since, say, 1790 has had the undivided allegiance of all the French people or even of nearly all.

The acceptance by almost everybody in Britain and the United States of the legitimacy of their rulers' authority has no parallel in France. The events of 1940-45, the ambiguous title on the one hand of the Vichy regime and on the other of the "Resistance," merely deepened divisions already deep. And it is not only a matter of division, for the French revolutionary tradition is in itself a weapon that the French Communists and their Russian rulers can and do use.

There are many reasons why so many millions of Frenchmen and Frenchwomen vote the Communist ticket, but one is traditional: it is the duty of the workers, of the "people," in the exclusive French sense of the term, to be "on the Left," to be for "the Revolution" and the Communist party, which by sleight of hand and by claims that are not totally fictitious, has managed to take over the assets vested in the revolutionary tradition.

Those assets are very considerable. For the French Revolution is still psychologically going on. It is hard for Americans to realize this; their revolution is over and done with. The American Revolution recalls less such radical demagogues as Sam Adams and Tom Paine than the "Daughters" stanchly defending not the *status quo* so much as an *ante status quo*. And for the Frenchman with sentimental attachments to the "Left," the United States is well represented by the Daughters of the American Revolution; the United States is seen, that is to say, as the bulwark of "reaction."

The average American will think this is nonsense; it is, but nonsense is a fact of life. And the French have, far less than any other people in Western Europe, little first-hand knowledge of America. There is no equivalent for the mass knowledge of the United States to be found in Britain, Italy or Germany. And the picture of the United States drawn by writers like Sartre and Simone de Beauvoir represents very well the kind of non-knowledge that the French have.

Lastly, France needs a new revolution in another sense. It needs to be made into a modern industrial power if it is not to decline to the status of Spain. Many Frenchmen think that this cannot be done in the terms of traditional democracy, that the United States, deliberately or not, is bolstering up an economic system that needs a complete reform which no parliamentary system is likely to produce.

The people who think this way are not necessarily either Communists or fellow-travelers. They may be very "anti-Soviet," but they are also likely to be anti-American. That the reconstruction of France has gained greatly from American aid, that the recent loan to the Schuman plan pool is an earnest of American intelligent good will, that to think of the American "capitalist" system in terms of French "capitalism" is merely silly; all these truths are true but they are not in wide enough circulation.

On these French fears, traditions, illusions, the Communists can play and do play skillfully. They can revive memories of the German terror to offset the threat of the Russian terror; they can play on the fears of the *petits bourgeois* threatened and rightly threatened by a modernization of the French economy.

The Communists can exploit every American error in tact or judgment; they can help to make France nearly ungovernable. They have strong cards and they often, though not always, play them well.

Compared with France, Britain is a much more reliable ally. Indeed, only senators talking without reflecting can really think that if America needs allies at all, she can do without Britain or replace her by Formosa, Siam, South Korea and the like.

But as an ally, Britain has her own liabilities. Like France, she is conscious of past glories and past power.

True, the United States did not supplant Britain out of ambition or ill will. True, American policy to Britain in recent years has been on the whole generous as well as wise. But it is expecting too much of human nature to expect the British to like their changed status.

They think, or many of them think, that somehow or other the United States did well out of a war that ruined or nearly ruined Britain. That immense quantities of American wealth, steel, wool, cotton, were expended in the immense waste of war; that, more precious still, the lives of hundreds of thousands of Americans were spent; that American wealth is the joint result of American resources and American industry and skill, are all truths that many millions do not accept, perhaps because they are not reiterated enough. That American power is a beneficent reality, the only barrier between Britain and enslavement to Russia, is a truth more generally accepted, but often sulkily accepted. . . .

Lastly there are the Americans. A Kremlin list of objectives, in ascending order of desirability, would put making the people of the United States disgusted with the alliance and their chief allies at the top. With American withdrawal from Europe or widespread hostility to the burdens of the alliance in America, Western Europe would, in no long time, be ripe for plucking and the United States encircled. So, in fact, the American attitude is basic; even more important than the French or British.

What risks does the alliance run in America? I find it hard to estimate. But many Americans, at any rate many Americans over forty, still find it difficult, I think, to accept the fact that America needs allies at all. They are obviously a nuisance; they are costly, ungrateful, disorderly. They are more trouble than they are worth.

This view involves an overestimate even of American power and an underestimate of American danger. . . .

But this dwindling group is less important than the larger and not necessarily dwindling group that finds the price of having allies too high. It is not primarily a matter of money or forces stationed overseas. It is a matter of having to consider the fears, doubts and interests of allies. There is the old American tradition (baseless, as far as I know) that Americans are always being outsmarted by foreigners. How dangerous then is an alliance when the outsmarting goes on continuously!

It is also a matter of believing that America is both infallible and nearly, or quite, omnipotent. In that case, negotiation, with enemies or allies, is wrong. It is, or should be, a matter of telling them. If they don't like it, they can lump it. And there is a more rational conviction that as America's allies simply can't do without her, they will have to like it. That the English and French might be prodded into disastrous irrationality is a possibility that is ignored; that the alliance might continue formally in being, but with its heart taken out of it and most of its utility gone, is also a possibility that is ignored. . . .

And lastly, there is a far more widespread and respectable emotion—as respectable as the French and British resentment of their decline in status, but not more rational. The American people have reason to feel deceived by the results of the last war, in which they were the chief instruments of victory, but which simply removed one menace to replace it by another, and one whose present power is, in part, the result of American mistakes—and American generosity.

This is a most unpleasant world that they unconsciously helped to make; they resent it and they resent, more or less consciously, the alliance as evident proof of the failure of victory to bring security and as the most obvious example of the price that has to be paid for that failure.

The millions who feel this way are not hostile to the alliance; they are often willing to pay the full price, but they resent the price and they pay sulkily. And that sulky attitude, met by sulky attitudes in France and Britain, might produce an alienation of the peoples which would undermine the alliance.

What can be done to underpin it? Some things are out of anybody's power. I can't see the schism in French society being cured by French or American or British policies. I can't see the French and British weariness being cured immediately, but it can be cured in time. I can't see the American people, notoriously not the most patient of peoples, learning quickly the arts of negotiation from strength, or ceasing to resent the fact that America now is vulnerable and part of a very dangerous world.

But there are certain things that can be done and should be done. Another and more favorable picture of America could be put across. . . . The dilettante attitude to politics that lies behind so much intellectual anti-Americanism can be shown up for what it is—a retreat into an ivory basement, *not* a courageous taking of a position. The longer the alliance lasts (provided the hostile forces are not given undue aid and comfort), the more natural it begins to look. Already, NATO is more part of the landscape than it was even a year or two ago. There is bone where there was only gristle. There is not yet enough bone, but that will come. . . .

And, I think, we may count on the cooperation of the Soviet government to remind us all from time to time that we are in danger and what kind of danger we are in.

It would be so easy for the Soviet government to lull the credulous to sleep, to dope the people who think that receiving the Comédie Français in Moscow with one of the best organized displays of spontaneous enthusiasm since the collapse of the Axis means peace. But truth will out; the rulers of Russia cannot, apparently, *feel* the outside world; they will, I think, provide object lessons every year or so.

And there may grow up in all the allied nations an understanding of what enlightened self-interest dictates. This is better than mere common fear or better than the transient emotion, gratitude. And here the lead must come from the most powerful people. The American people should remember the old saying, "Do a man a good turn and he will never forgive you." He is even less likely to forgive you if you keep on telling him you are doing him a good turn and much more likely to forgive and forget if you make it plain that you are primarily interested in doing yourself a good turn; only secondarily in doing a good turn to someone else. When each nation, as well as each government, feels this and acts on it, then we shall be well on the way to that "more perfect union" of which the alliance is a prefiguration.

FRANCE'S POSTWAR FOREIGN POLICY [2]

The foreign affairs of the Fourth Republic up to 1954 can be not too arbitrarily divided into three periods of three years each. In each of these periods France has pursued a distinctive policy which, though successful for a while, ultimately ended in failure. Each time French objectives have had to be abandoned far short of their

[2] From "The Twilight of French Foreign Policy," by Edgar S. Furniss, Jr., a member of the Department of Politics at Princeton University. *Yale Review.* 44:64-80. Autumn 1954. Copyright 1954 by Yale University Press. Reprinted by permission.

goals because of an interaction of external and internal events over which France could not or would not exert effective control. The difficulties in which France has recurrently found herself have lain not only in the general international situation, which, until 1950, was steadily deteriorating, but also in the inadequate French response to the exigencies of that situation.

The First Phase

As soon as Paris and most of France had been cleared of Germans in 1944, the Provisional French Government of Charles de Gaulle embarked upon a policy of gaining recognition by the other Allies of France's claim to be one of the great powers. While this might be called a policy of prestige, it was based on the very practical proposition that only by being admitted to the councils of the mighty could France participate in decisions vitally affecting her. . . .

One reason France wanted recognition as a great power was her desire to use her influence to serve as mediator between the Soviet Union and the Anglo-American nations. French leaders were among the first to detect the beginnings of the cold war. Having barely won one world war and scarcely survived a second, France would, they knew, be doomed by a third. Successful mediation not only would add to French importance; it was felt to be indispensable to French survival. The conception of France's role as mediator was stated by Bidault in the course of the Consultative Assembly's first debate on foreign policy, held in November 1944, immediately prior to the opening of negotiations concerning a Franco-Soviet Alliance. "An alliance with the West?" asked Bidault. "Of course. How could we do otherwise? But an alliance with the

East also. We are interested in affairs which reach beyond the confines of the West. France will never permit herself to be limited to the Western part of the world." In the words of André Siegfried, France "felt her mission to be that of serving as a moderating element, indispensable to the equilibrium between the great blocs that are trying to divide the world up between themselves." . . .

Even as late as 1947, when the policy of compromise had become virtually impossible, French Minister Bidault strenuously sought to gain Soviet acceptance of Secretary of State Marshall's proposal and thus remain with the West. To the National Assembly Bidault stated that the invitation sent to the Soviet Union to participate in a preliminary conference on American aid and European economic recovery was far from being *pro-forma,* but stemmed rather from a sincere desire to obtain agreement among Britain, France, and the Soviet Union before the smaller states were invited to join. In the Foreign Minister's statement can be seen the twin conceptions of France as a great power and France as a mediatory power, in this instance a *European* mediator between two partially European nations, Great Britain and the Soviet Union.

The attempt by France to play the role of mediator, to remain aloof from both the Eastern and Western camps, ended in failure. The primary reason for the failure, of course, was the growing gap between the United States and Great Britain, on the one hand, and the Soviet Union, on the other. The chasm ultimately became too wide to be bridged; France was forced despite her wishes to choose sides. At the same time, the Soviet Union threw France into the Anglo-American camp by such hostile maneuvers as its refusal to accede to French demands for more German coal, its rejection of the

Marshall Plan overtures, and its signaling for French Communists to combat the government of which they were nominally a part.

Of all the major powers', France's hopes of doing business with the Soviet Union remained alive the longest. The failure of those hopes was doubtless due in large part to developments in the international environment, but domestic causes were not lacking. The elementary requirements of a mediator in world politics are that it be able to dispose of considerable independent power with which to support its proposals, and that it occupy an intermediate position between the forces it is trying to bring together. At the end of 1947 France fulfilled neither of these criteria. De Gaulle's emphasis on France's prestige and grandeur had not been coupled with measures to recover the nation's economic strength. Initial failures in the economic field prepared the way for disastrous inflation. Controls, prematurely removed, could not once more be applied. Three years after the liberation the French economy, far from showing signs of recovery, was near the point of collapse. Behind the façade of grandeur lurked a tattered bankrupt.

Nor were political conditions much better. Against the urging of de Gaulle, the French had finally, in a spirit of lassitude following on heated argument, adopted a constitution making strong government possible only if the three largest French parties could agree to share power and to advocate a common program. Of these three parties—the Catholic Mouvement Républicain Populaire, the Socialist, and the Communist—the largest was the Communist. In a very real sense, then, French political stability depended upon the pursuit of domestic and foreign policies which would permit Communist collaboration within the executive branch. But by 1947 the Kremlin had given up hope of the French Communists' coming to power within the parliamentary framework and ordered them into opposition. Although Socialist Ramadier succeeded in the delicate task of removing the Communists from his entourage, the inherent weaknesses of the political structure of the Fourth Republic henceforth stood revealed.

Besides lacking sufficient domestic strength to back up her proposals, France had increasing difficulty in occupying a truly intermediate position between the two great blocs. Instead of being neutral territory, the country was becoming a battleground over which the Eastern and Western colossi fought, a battleground perhaps less dramatic than Italy only because the advantages of the West were greater in France. Long before the Marshall Plan was put into operation France had been forced to seek American aid, which by 1948 totaled almost $2 billion. Trips by French leaders to Washington became more rewarding than those to Moscow. As Bidault said, in contrast to Moscow's antagonism, he could return from Washington with "a little coal." In the last analysis the United States extended her assistance because she believed that France could be saved from Communist clutches and because she believed France was worth saving, meaning that France, as her statesmen repeatedly pointed out, was a Western country with a long history far antedating that of the United States as defender of Western civilization—in a word that France was not and could not be *between* West and East but was and belonged with the West. Much the same conclusion, as has just been mentioned, was reached by the Soviet Union. Having failed by only a narrow margin to bring France along the course followed by the "popular democracies" of Eastern Europe, Russia decided to fight the battle henceforth with subversion and sabotage. But these tactics catapulted

France into the Western camp, there to remain until and unless French conditions could be rendered so chaotic that the French Communist Party could seize power.

The Second Phase

Having been forced to choose the West, France quickly and deftly embarked on the second of its post-war foreign policies—a policy that was to dominate French actions in the years 1947-50. The essential ingredients were: first, domestic economic recovery with assistance from the Economic Cooperation Administration; second, enhancement of military security through alliances with other Western powers; third, leadership in promoting Western European unity; fourth, gradual admission of Occupied Germany to this Western European structure in such circumstances and on such terms that she would not become a menace to French security. Domestic economic recovery had been the objective of the Monnet Plan, set in motion in 1946, but it was only the transfusion of ECA dollars that enabled the plan to become more than a blueprint. By 1950, when the plan was nominally at an end and military considerations had superseded economic in American calculations regarding assistance, the French economy had made significant strides towards recovery. In many sectors production figures had surpassed totals attained in the last prewar year, 1938.

The structure of French military alliances was completed within two years by the signing of the Brussels Treaty and the North Atlantic Treaty. The former was something of a triumph for French diplomacy in respect both to the organizational requirements of the instrument and the participation of Great Britain. The Brussels Treaty provided for consultative committees to plan military and economic measures, and Great Britain, already allied to France under terms of the Dunkirk Treaty of 1947, was now committed to aid the European signators by all military and other means at its disposal in the event of an aggression by any power. Like the Monnet Plan, however, the Brussels Treaty could become truly effective only with American assistance. In April 1949 that assistance was assured with the signing of the North Atlantic Pact by twelve nations, including France and the United States. Not so precise and automatic in its provisions as the French would have liked, the treaty nonetheless contained the assurance that the United States regarded the security of Western Europe as indispensable to her own security. Equally important, the United States was now prepared to underwrite this proposition with military aid, with additional American troops stationed in Germany, and through leadership in the formation of a North Atlantic Treaty Organization with headquarters in France.

Although France was clearly dependent in the economic and military spheres on assistance from the United States, she was all the more determined to attain as much freedom of decision as possible. The events of 1945-47 had shown that she could not do this alone. Perhaps she could now do so as leader of a united Western Europe. This philosophy was clearly stated . . . by André Siegfried:

Between the two formidable masses of the United States and Soviet Russia thus exists a force, a third force, somewhat loosely organized and amorphous, but influential, however, by the consensus which it represents. . . . What unites them (the countries of Western Europe), in addition to an ancient land, is the tradition of a tested association, perhaps even more the hope of escaping the Communist embrace, if possible without putting themselves under too close a protection by the United States.

To be sure, intra-European machinery existed in such instruments as the Organization for European Economic Cooperation and the European Payments Union, but France wanted far more. Her leaders seized on the initiative taken by such private groups as that proposing a United States of Europe, to which British Opposition Leader Winston Churchill had lent his great prestige and support. The French were also encouraged by a speech of British Foreign Minister Ernest Bevin calling for a Western Union. With both British parties seemingly behind the idea, the French were emboldened to propose that the consultative structure of the Brussels Pact work out the details of a European Union. Less than a year later, on May 5, 1947, the Statute of Europe was signed. Although considerably short of the supranational goal set by France, the instrument was ratified by the National Assembly in only two months, blinding speed for that body.

Another reason for the sense of urgency on the part of the French in the creation of a strong Western European organization was the rise of West Germany. By the time the Marshall Plan came into operation, France had been most reluctantly forced to abandon all her original occupation objectives in Germany. The Rhineland-Ruhr industrial center was not to be detached from Germany; Germany was not to be broken up into small, autonomous states held together by the loosest of ties; in short, Germany could no longer be treated as a defeated, dangerous enemy. More positively stated, American pressure had forced France to follow the policy of German recovery in order that Germany could contribute to the anti-Soviet coalition then in formation. Admitting that occupation controls should be relaxed to permit Germany to recapture its economic and political strength, France was confronted with the problem of lessening the attendant danger to her own security. The French solution was to seek to link West Germany indissolubly with a united Europe, the leadership of which was most clearly French. To this end Germany was admitted to the Council of Europe, but the capstone to this policy was French Foreign Minister Robert Schuman's proposal for a coal and steel pool with Germany. Defending his truly revolutionary idea in the National Assembly in July, 1950, Schuman said, "We want to make any war between France and Germany not only impossible, but materially impossible."

Despite the successes which attended French foreign policy in the years 1947-1950, the close of 1950 found the objectives of that policy unreached. Worse, France could no longer move in the same direction. Once again, the trouble resulted from a combination of external and internal factors, which France could not or would not manipulate to her own advantage. The menace against which France and other Western nations were preparing had been revealed by such Soviet actions as the seizure of Czechoslovakia and the blockade of Berlin, but because no overt aggression had been involved in either action, it appeared that the menace was a general one without a specific date of maximum danger. From these illusions the anti-Soviet coalition was awakened when the North Korean armies crossed the Thirty-Eighth Parallel in June 1950. Scarcely assimilating the first shock, the West sustained a second and worse one when the Chinese Communists intervened in time to rescue North Korea from defeat. It now appeared that military aggression was most definitely on the agenda of international communism, that the menace to Western Europe was specific and immediate. Responding to the danger, the North Atlantic Treaty Organization demanded greater sacrifices from all its members, including France, in order that

Western military power in the immediate future might be formidable enough to deter the Soviet Union from aggression in Europe. The United States, working towards the same end, reversed the original order of priority between economic and military assistance for Western Europe, to place heavier and heavier emphasis on military aid. Finally, and most important of all, the United States judged that even a stepped-up program would leave NATO forces dangerously weak and accordingly proposed that West Germany be rearmed to help fill the yawning gap between Western and Eastern military power in Europe.

The condition of France was such that she could not resist these new pressures. Though the state of the economy was greatly improved over that of 1948, recovery was far from complete at the formal expiration of the Monnet Plan in 1950. . . . Even with large-scale military assistance from the United States, French rearmament on the scale now posited by NATO could be achieved only at the expense of heavy economic sacrifices —which it was doubtful the nation could support.

Nor was the structure of Western Europe which France had been building complete enough or strong enough to carry the burden of the new emergency. Adamant British opposition to any European federation had made of the Council of Europe little more than a debating society, whose many resolutions and recommendations were not put into practice by the various national governments. The French had urged the British to reconsider their first negative reaction to the Schuman Plan, but the reconsidered response was a douse of cold water on French enthusiasm for a united Europe.

Without British participation in a truly supranational body, the structure of Europe was not strong enough, in the French view, to support a rearmed Germany. Previous French policy had been based on the gradual admission of Western Germany into European councils. . . . But no provision had been made for a rearmed Germany. As late as May 1950, General Clay's address in New York calling for the right of Germans to contribute to their own defense had been answered by French leaders in most emphatic terms. Speaking the same day at Reims, President Auriol declared that the French had paid for previous German actions in blood and could admit of no rearmament, while three days later Minister of National Defense René Pleven replied to a question in the Council of the Republic that if Clay's position represented the views of the American government, he would resign. One month later came Korea; four months later Clay's position did indeed become that of American officials. Out of French weakness, French ingenuity was forced to produce a new policy.

The Third Phase

This new policy, which guided French action from 1950 to 1954 . . . [was] dominated by the problem of German rearmament. Clearly the objective was to postpone as long as possible the date on which that rearmament would be authorized, to retard after that the actual process of rearmament, and, finally, to hedge German rearmament about with as many restrictions as possible. . . .

The delay . . . [was] used to devise various formulas to lessen the impact on France of German rearmament. When the first formula, a truly united Europe on the political level, was not realized in the Council of Europe, French pressure for a political community was channeled into the Assembly of the Coal-Steel Pool. There a draft constitution for a European Political Community took shape during 1952 and was revised and further debated in 1953. The Political Community was designed as a roof to shelter not only the Defense Community, but the Coal-Steel Pool [see next article "Toward European Union"—Ed.] and such other *ad hoc* economic arrangements as the proposed "Green" or Agricultural Pool, the Transport Pool, Health Pool, etc. In the meantime, however, the only supranational organization actually emerging from a blueprint to an operating stage was the Coal-Steel Pool itself. Early in 1953 the Pool, having been accepted by the six countries of Western Europe—Belgium, Netherland, Luxembourg, France, Italy, and West Germany—began limited operations. From the French standpoint this was a major triumph for its foreign policy. As and if the Pool organization moves along its projected path towards control over Western European coal and steel production, distribution, and marketing, a new series of ties will be forged, making ever more difficult unilateral action by West Germany. . . .

Two propositions about West Germany have by now become clear, propositions which set at naught French diplomatic activity over the past . . . [few years]. First, the Germans will be rearmed. There will be a German army, whether under the auspices of the European Defense Community (whose provisions now call for German units far larger than the French first proposed as the only safe size) or under the North Atlantic Treaty Organization (where little control over the number and equipment of German soldiers will be exerted) or bi-laterally, as the result of agreements between the United States and the West German Republic. [See "Partial text of the London and Paris Agreements," in this section, below.—Ed.] None of these solutions is satisfactory to the French because—and this is the second proposition that is now clear—efforts to create a European Political Community through the Coal-Steel Pool . . . [have proved] no more successful than earlier efforts to build a federal Council of Europe. Domestic weakness is causing leadership in Western Europe to slip from France's hands, thus duplicating the sorry experience of the interwar period.

The French Army is not large enough to carry out commitments in Western Europe—the most important and least mentioned of which is to be more powerful than the contingents West Germany could muster—and . . . [still] hold together the crumbling French Empire. . . . At the same time, pressure mounts to lighten the armament burden. Domestic resources are desperately needed to cover the demands of the French people for improved living standards, the demands of the French state for a balanced budget, and the demands of a world market in which French goods are considerably overpriced in relation to those of France's competitors. The French are apparently unwilling and unable to order their economy in effective fashion, whether the form of organization be private ownership, state ownership, or partnership between the state and private individuals. . . .

French weakness provides a pitiable contrast to West German strength. Because of its phenomenal economic recovery, aided, be it noted, by the former occupying powers and by the happy requirements that no money be spent on armaments, West Germany has been able to seize the leadership in Western Europe from France. It is now German leaders who talk of the need for Western European unity, and as they do so, the opposition to concrete measures promoting such unity grows greater in France. What is the advantage in having a European army if it is going to be dominated by Germans? Why surrender national sovereignty to a political community in which Germany's will be the strongest voice? Why take measures to reduce trade barriers when such measures will enable German products to control the market? German trade competition has become so serious that the British would like to see their competitor shoulder its share of the armament burden, but to the French this cure appears far worse than the disease. Inside or outside the framework of European organizations, then, German economic and military superiority over France seems assured. The result has been highly ironical: increased French opposition to the very goal of Western European unity that had been a hallmark of French diplomacy since 1947.

The twilight of French foreign policy is at hand. After previous reverses French diplomacy came up with new ideas, new objectives, new programs that promised much for the country. In the execution of these programs some successes were attained, but the net result was failure. . . Only with increasing difficulty can France continue her claim to being a major nation with world-wide commitments and world-wide power.

TOWARD EUROPEAN UNION [3]

The first question to ask ourselves is why attempts to organize Europe failed before 1948. In 1930 Aristide Briand wrote a memorandum which called for a pact to bring about a "European Association"—the first time that the question of unity was officially raised. But the Briand proposal confined itself mainly to outlining a legal structure, in particular a system of arbitration. An economic aim—the establishment of a common market— was suggested only summarily. More important still, any infringement upon national sovereignty was definitely

[3] From "France and Europe," by Robert Schuman, French Foreign Minister, 1948-1952, and French Premier, 1947-1948. *Foreign Affairs*. 31:349-60. April 1953. Reprinted by permission. Copyright by the Council on Foreign Relations, Inc.

excluded. In thus making it a matter of principle that not a particle of their sovereignty was to be relinquished the signatories would have promised to deprive themselves of the chief means of achieving their goal. It was to be accepted in advance that the proposed organization would be powerless.

The plan had no practical result. But even if the French government had suggested limiting sovereignty, it still would have had no chance of success, for no European country was ready for the concept of a supranational authority. The idea was not acceptable to a man like Poincaré, and still less to a Mussolini; and though Great Britain and the Scandinavian countries had rallied to an international organization of the traditional type, there was no chance that they would go beyond that. The French plan was stillborn because it was ahead of its time, and even if it had been tried, it would not have worked. . . .

At the end of the Second World War the situation was entirely different. This time there could be no doubt that Germany had suffered a crushing military defeat. Ravaged by war, fully occupied by Allied troops, the country was in a state of political collapse, without either an army or a central government. She could get back to her feet only with the aid of the Allies. Moreover, the regime imposed by the Soviets in their zone of occupation did not attract the German people as a whole. . . .

In 1947 the Western Allies became aware of Russia's military threat, evidenced by the network of twenty-seven treaties binding her satellites to her. At the same time Moscow rejected the collective aid offered to Europe under the Marshall Plan. It was plain that the Russians intended to install themselves firmly in the heart of Europe, and to retain a free hand to spread their domination over the Western part of it by propaganda and intrigue.

The three other Allies soon countered this move. To allocate and put to work the funds made available by the Marshall Plan they created, in April 1948, the first permanent pan-European organization—the OEEC [Organization for European Economic Cooperation]. Under the threat of danger, and prompted and encouraged by generous assistance from America, Europeans began to acquire a consciousness of "Europe." Whereas the Treaty of Dunkirk, concluded between Great Britain and France on March 4, 1947, had been directed primarily against a possible German menace, the Brussels Treaty of March 17, 1948, laid the basis for cooperation among five countries, and the London Agreements of June 1948 inaugurated a constructive policy toward Germany. [As later revised and extended to include Germany and Italy, the Treaty became a substitute for the European Defense Community after the French rejection of EDC. See "Partial text of London and Paris Agreements," in this section, below.—Ed.]

This change of direction called for new methods, and it was then that France played her full part in organizing Europe. Up to that time, cooperation had always been confined to agreements between governments, operating under the rule of unanimity. Since each contracting power had the right of veto, action often became impossible. Before anything effective could be done, the dogma of national sovereignty had to be breached. The way had been cleared by private groups which had worked energetically to popularize the idea of an authority above that of any single state. This idea found expression in the preamble to the French constitution of 1946. In August 1948 the French and Belgian governments . . . called a conference to study whether some sort of political tie among all the European countries was practicable, and this conference (consisting at first of representatives of the five countries of the Brussels Treaty) met at Brussels on October 25, 1948. Here the dispersed efforts of all the private groups were gathered together in the "European Movement."

Though differences quickly emerged, twelve governments signed the Constitution of the Council of Europe on May 5, 1949—one month after the signing of the Atlantic Pact. Here was something new. It was not a committee of foreign ministers bound to reach unanimous decisions, but for the first time a permanent assembly common to twelve countries, with parliamentary delegates who voted individually and not as members of an instructed delegation. This assembly has consultative powers only, but it draws authority from the fact that it can give free voice to the diverse opinions held in the participating nations, thus embodying a European spirit and creating a permanent relationship among the most representative men of these countries. The work done by committees provides an opportunity for thorough study of the delegates' ideas, and for preparation of recommendations to governments.

In 1949 a German Federal Parliament was elected and formed the first government at Bonn. On April 1, 1950, West Germany was invited to join the Council of Europe, with full constitutional rights as soon as the Western Allies had restored its sovereignty over the conduct of foreign relations. Germany's entrance into the Council of Strasbourg was the first recognition of her right to join an international organization. It was in keeping with the development of the occupation regime into a contractual arrangement, negotiated between the three occupying powers and the German Federal Government.

On the basis of this broad European policy West Germany reentered the community of free peoples. Only Europe as such could have provided the practical machinery for such a move. It could not have been done through the United Nations, where a Soviet veto would have interposed, nor under the Atlantic Pact, which presupposes the existence of an army. The integration of Germany with Europe was one of the primary aims of French foreign policy. From the beginning, the effort to organize Europe had had a double purpose: first, to strengthen the European countries, which if left to fend for themselves would be condemned to political and economic dissolution; and second, to bring Germany into the common endeavors so that she would not repeat her former errors. A democratic Germany on an equal footing with the other members of the European community will have no excuse for rebellion, aloofness and dreams of conquest and domination.

Participation in the Council of Europe was the first step in this direction, but it was not enough and France did not hesitate to take another. She envisaged the creation of such strong organic bonds among the European nations—Germany in particular included—that no German Government could break them, and the establishment of a living and permanent community that would put an end to old antagonisms and usher in an era of profitable collaboration. Such a community must be based on mutual good faith and confidence—and that is possible only if all members find it to their interest to keep faith with the others, recognizing that what promotes the common advantage will promote their individual welfare.

In a solemn declaration on May 9, 1950, France proposed to Germany and the other European countries that they put their production of coal and steel under an authority independent both of governments and private interests. For the first time in history there was to be an agency above national parliaments and private business which would reach its decisions in consultation with producers, workers and political bodies and which would be responsible only to an assembly representing the participating powers. Thus we hoped that considerations of narrow national interest would be replaced by regard for the common interest, that national antagonisms would be transcended, and that, since none of the partners had control of its own coal and steel, war among them would be unthinkable. The objective was to remove the danger of war between rival nations and to develop a community spirit which would not weaken national attachments but provide a wider basis for new activities and new goals. Such a community would also be able to solve problems which arise from the uneven distribution of natural resources and technical skills.

Within ten months the treaty was drawn up and signed, and on August 10, 1952, it became effective among the six signatory Powers. Since February 10 . . . [1953] there has been a single market for coal and iron ore in Western Europe, and . . . steel will also move freely among these six countries [Belgium, the Netherlands, France, Germany, and Luxembourg] without customs duties of any kind. Their total population, incidentally, is almost exactly that of the United States. The unification of Europe is irrevocably under way. The treaty is due to run for fifty years, and though it is limited to two industries they are ones which are essential for every national economy. The territory to which it applies is also limited; yet it includes half of free Europe —the part of Europe which in the past has been most often at war. We have gone beyond the stage of talk and theory and shown what we want to do and can do.

It may be instructive, at this point, to analyze the conditions under which the plan evolved and was brought to completion. At first it created some astonishment in France, but in general the French people were pleased to see that their government had taken the lead in European affairs. The next stage was one of increasing worry about the danger of "omnipotent technocracy," that is, the fear that Germany would escape from all restrictions and dominate the other partners. A campaign, at times very violent, was unleashed against the plan. The chief manufacturers' association led the attack, while labor unions rallied to the defense. Meanwhile, lawyers dissected the text of the treaty and economists pointed out all the risks —all of which made a great impression on the French parliament. But public opinion looked upon the idea as a practical attempt to end the threat of war and strengthen a divided Europe; and, as a result of this public support, the treaty was ratified by an unforeseen majority: in the National Assembly by a vote of 377 to 233, and in the Senate by a vote of 177 to 31, with 87 abstentions. Once ratification was settled, hostility died down and all interested parties gave the plan their loyal support. The intractable enemies are the Communists, who cannot conceive of a European policy not dictated by Moscow.

In Germany, the plan met with a warm welcome from the governmental majority, and the Bonn parliament approved it by a vote of 232 to 143. Chancellor Adenauer had given it his support from the beginning, just as he had supported with his strong convictions and powerful personality the general trend toward solutions of individual problems on a European basis. He has set himself against the nationalism which twice led Germany to disaster; but, like every leader in a democracy, he has to reckon with public opinion, play for time and take precautions. . . . West Germany has not given up the hope of unity, and is all the more anxious for that very reason to regain its sovereignty and establish its security. Farsighted Germans know that only the integration of Europe can achieve this double objective for them in the foreseeable future.

THE ORIGINS OF EDC [4]

The European Defense Community originally was proposed by the French. Its purpose was to prevent West Germany from having a national army. Even so, its provisions immediately encountered strong opposition within France.

Because of this, it was kept out of the limelight. . . .

[It] was furiously attacked from the beginning by the Communists and, for different reasons, by General Charles de Gaulle. Few of those who defended it were vigorous in its praises. Many declared that, while it was not what they wanted, it was the best France could get.

The idea was an outgrowth of the United States demand for the arming of West Germany that was introduced in the North Atlantic Council shortly after the outbreak of the Korean war.

One month earlier in Strasbourg Prime Minister Churchill had suggested to the Council of Europe the formation of a European army. His suggestion was supported by Paul Reynaud, former Premier of France, and they together presented the motion that resulted in the first discussion of the plan.

[4] From "Project for EDC Begun in France," by Lansing Warren, correspondent for the New York *Times*. New York *Times*. p 10. August 31, 1954. Reprinted by permission.

Jean Monnet, who was working on the European Coal and Steel Community, took up the question and the defense community project developed into a corollary plan.

Behind this suggestion was the basic idea of fostering peace in Europe by an agreement between West Germany and France. It was thus that René Pleven, then Premier, proposed the European Defense Community, and got the approval of the National Assembly to suggest the plan to other European nations in October 1950.

As then drafted by the French, it was a different and a far less ambitious plan than the one eventually incorporated in the treaty. It proposed to arm the West Germans only as "combat teams" and would have prohibited the Germans from using heavy arms or having a general staff or high command.

France invited all the European nations to join in the defense community, but only Belgium, the Netherlands, Luxembourg, Italy and West Germany agreed to take part. The first conference, held in February, broke down without agreement and it was not until January 1952 that a compromise was reached.

This proposed that West Germany should be allowed to form divisions with its own officers, but would participate in the Atlantic alliance only indirectly through its presence in a European army. West Germany's army was to be controlled by its association and its merger with the forces of the six other European nations.

Though the treaty was signed May 27, 1952, the French soon afterward demanded the addition of a series of protocols, which were accepted by the partners at a meeting held in Rome in February 1953.

In July of that year the treaty was first ratified by the lower house of parliament in the Netherlands.

Meanwhile West Germany's rapid economic recovery was reviving French misgivings, and fears that a six-nation community would be dominated by the Germans. Without explanation Robert Schuman, the then Foreign Minister, and Antoine Pinay, then the Premier, put the treaty "on ice."

Under Premier Joseph Laniel some timid efforts were made to get an indirect expression from the Assembly but the Government never dared to take the risk of pressing for a decision.

It was not until Pierre Mendès-France took office that a definite promise was given. M. Mendès-France declared he would get the question settled one way or the other before the National Assembly adjourned for its summer recess.

Finally he obtained French agreement to the excessive and ill-fated protocols rejected in Brussels. M. Mendès-France then put the problem to the Assembly, which, in effect, killed the treaty [in a vote taken on August 30, 1954].

IMMEDIATE U.S. REACTION TO
THE DEFEAT OF EDC [5]

The cause of Western defense and European unification suffered a staggering blow when a leaderless, hamstrung and confused French National Assembly in effect rejected the European Defense Community treaty last night and thereby killed, at least for the present, the most promising Western enterprise of the postwar era. The death blow, in the shape of a procedural motion to break off debate on the treaty and postpone its ratifica-

[5] "Defeat for EDC," editorial. New York *Times.* p20. August 31, 1954. Reprinted by permission.

tion indefinitely, was approved by a vote of 319 to 264, which means that a change in less than thirty votes would have had a different result.

Four of the prospective members of the European Defense Community, which provides for a unified European Army with German divisions in it and for supranational institutions to promote further European unification, have already ratified the treaty and a fifth was about to do so. But there were simply not enough "Europeans" in the French National Assembly to do likewise, and for the life of the present Assembly the project is now regarded as dead.

This is a development that marks the greatest postwar triumph for Soviet policy, which made the destruction of the European Defense Community one of its main objectives in order to wean Germany from the West and open the road to a further Communist advance in Europe. There is no doubt that it could have, in Secretary Dulles' words, the most "serious consequences."

It is a particularly heavy blow to Chancellor Adenauer and his policy of German integration with the West. Unless quickly softened, it could precipitate in Germany a feeling of rejection and frustration leading to a resurgence of German nationalism and increased pressure for a new "Rapallo" approach to Soviet Russia that would make a democratic unification of Europe impossible. [The 1922 Treaty of Rapallo between Germany and Soviet Russia provided for economic and political cooperation.—Ed.]

But the same development is also a heavy blow to American policy in Europe. This policy, in keeping with NATO Council decisions, called not only for a German contribution to Western defense but also for European unification to eliminate any possibility of future war between France and Germany as an essential condition of Western defense and the security of our troops in Europe. The action of the French National Assembly, which destroys the basis of this policy, now releases the United States and Britain from all pledges regarding the stationing of troops on the Continent and may, indeed, lead to the "agonizing reappraisal" of both American policy and NATO troop dispositions Mr. Dulles has foreshadowed.

The causes for this melancholy result of a four-year effort lie deeply imbedded in the French character and political structure. But the primary responsibility for it must now rest on Premier Mendès-France, who refused to fight for the Community project and even failed to force a direct vote on the treaty itself. This, however, is not the end. M. Mendès-France himself has recognized that neither German sovereignty nor German rearmament can be delayed indefinitely, and many alternative plans for both are already under way. And the idea of European unification will live and flower when the present wreckers of it have sunk into oblivion.

TWO VIEWS ON THE FRENCH REJECTION OF EDC [6]

I

Premier Pierre Mendès-France, who had handled the Indo-China war, Tunisian autonomy and internal economic problems so brilliantly, came a cropper on the European Defense Community. Here he blundered and abdicated the leadership that is expected of a governmental leader.

[6] From "French Policy: Right or Wrong?" by (I) Herbert L. Matthews, editorial writer for the New York *Times*, and (II) Saul K. Padover, dean of the School of Politics, New School for Social Research, New York. *Foreign Policy Bulletin*. 34:20-2. October 15, 1954. Reprinted by permission.

Looking back, it seems like a case of defeatism. M. Mendès-France never liked the EDC and had obviously not taken the trouble to study it before he became premier. His chief feeling about it had been irritation that the subject should be allowed to divide French public and parliamentary opinion so sharply and that nothing ever seemed to be done about it. When he became premier he pledged his government to get a decision one way or another.

This was laudable, but he had not calculated the importance of the issue to Europe and America. The situation had reached a point, after two years of French procrastination and growing German strength, where something positive had to be done. In all likelihood this was going to be the last chance to get West Germany to accept something less than full sovereignty and full equality. Secretary of State John Foster Dulles had warned about an "agonizing reappraisal" a long time before. The United States policy on Europe had been sold to Americans, rightly or wrongly, as a part of a great new movement for European unity. The Benelux countries and West Germany had already ratified the treaty after much heart-searching and could not be asked to go back to their parliaments for a different treaty.

The one thing that was clear amidst the confusion was that rejection of the EDC by France would have catastrophic effects.

In that situation Premier Mendès-France started from the premise that the EDC as it stood would be defeated in the National Assembly. He therefore drew up protocols changing it to suit the opponents and in so doing alienated the supporters. The protocols were such that the Benelux countries and West Germany could not accept them without resubmitting the treaty to their parliaments. It was not made sufficiently clear that this was a bargaining position, and the French proposals were quickly rejected.

At this point leadership was in order. M. Mendès-France, however, was still convinced that there was no majority for the EDC in the National Assembly, and he washed his hands of the whole affair. If there had been any possibility of victory the premier had played his cards so badly that defeat was inevitable.

The sequel showed that the international situation had not been correctly gauged, for, according to all accounts, Premier Mendès-France and his supporters felt, at the time, quite pleased with the result and thought that now they could get on to other work and sooner or later evolve another plan for Western defense.

Then, as we know, things began to happen; and that was where United States policy on France suddenly shot off at a tangent. The "agonizing reappraisal" turned out to be a promise of complete sovereignty and full equality for West Germany, with France at first not even consulted. . . .

II

Little effort is being made to explain, if not to defend, the French position on EDC and on Germany. But whether we like it or not, there is a French position and a French argument.

At the outset this writer wants to make it clear that he is not a spokesman for France or a defender of its policies. Nor does he consider France's recent course necessarily wise. His primary interest is elucidation of a subject that is of momentous importance not only for the United States and France but for the whole free world.

To begin with, what is really surprising about the whole EDC crisis is America's surprise. For a long time objective observers of the French political scene have been reporting that EDC had little chance of passing the parliament and that hostility to Germany still ran deep. In a Foreign Policy Association Headline Series book, *Europe's Quest for Unity,* published a year and a half ago, this writer stated: "As 1953 opened, it was doubtful whether the French National Assembly would ratify EDC." The reasons for that were obvious to everybody who bothered to study France's situation. Nevertheless, the rejection of EDC shocked official Washington. One wonders whether we are dealing here with faulty intelligence or unstable psychology.

Secondly, it should be stressed that it is childish and unjust to blame Mendès-France for the EDC debacle. It was not France's premier but its public opinion that defeated the measure. Despite the fact that he well knew that a majority of Frenchmen were hostile to EDC, Mendès-France had the courage to bring the matter to a vote in the National Assembly and thereby once and for all clear the murky atmosphere. Four of his predecessors in the premiership, including those who had helped to create EDC, had lacked the courage to do so. They must bear a heavy load of the blame for having misled both Americans and Germans with unrealistic promises and interpretations.

Why did France reject EDC? The reasons are many and complex; they are political, emotional, psychological and economic. But cutting through the cross currents, one discerns three main causes.

First and foremost is the continuing fear of Germany. . . .

In the second place, there is the question of Great Britain. The French might have swallowed the EDC pill if they had had the British with them. British membership in EDC would have reassured the French and allayed their fears of the Germans; it would have balanced an equal number of British divisions against German ones, and so France would not have felt itself alone with its ancient enemy. This explains Mendès-France's hurried and urgent visit to Churchill on the eve of the EDC vote. But for reasons of their own the British refused to join EDC. To the French this was most galling. Here were the British, potentially in the same dangerous and exposed position as themselves, urging them to give up part of their most vital sovereignty—control of their armed forces—but refusing to do so themselves. There is no doubt that Britain's aloofness from EDC gave the project its *coup de grâce*.

Finally, there is Mendès-France's own estimate of the world situation. He did not throw his weight and that of his office for or against EDC, primarily because he no longer considered it of supreme importance. In common with many other unemotional observers of world politics he does not believe that the Communist danger is basically military. He thinks the Communist problem is essentially economic and political; hence, in his eyes military measures like EDC are insufficient. Fundamentally, what deters a possible Russian aggression is American thermonuclear power. This being the case, Mendès-France believes that France should devote its energies to making itself economically strong and healthy. With American power as a shelter, the French premier acts on the assumption that his country's military efforts can be safely subordinated to pressing economic reforms, the lack of which encourages communism within France.

PARTIAL TEXT OF THE LONDON AND
PARIS AGREEMENTS [7]

The conference of the nine powers, Belgium, Canada, France, German Federal Republic, Italy, Luxembourg, Netherlands, United Kingdom of Great Britain and Northern Ireland and United States, met in London from September 28 to October 3 [1954]. It dealt with the most important issues facing the Western world, security and European integration within the framework of a developing Atlantic community dedicated to peace and freedom. In this connection the conference considered how to assure the full association of the German Federal Republic with the West and the German defense contribution. . . .

Text

The governments of France, the United Kingdom and the United States declare that their policy is to end the occupation regime in the Federal Republic as soon as possible, to revoke the Occupation Statute and to abolish the Allied High Commission. The three governments will continue to discharge certain responsibilities in Germany arising out of the international situation.

It is intended to conclude, and to bring into force as soon as the necessary parliamentary procedures have been completed, the appropriate instruments for these purposes. General agreement has already been reached on the content of these instruments and representatives of the four governments will meet in the very near future to complete the final texts. The agreed arrangements may be put into effect either before or simultane-

[7] From "Text of the Final Act of Nine-Power Conference Held in London Between September 28 and October 3 [1954]." New York *Times*. p5. October 4, 1954. Reprinted by permission.

ously with the arrangements for the German defense contribution.

As these arrangements will take a little time to complete, the three governments have in the meantime issued the following declaration of intent:

Recognizing that a great country can no longer be deprived of the rights properly belonging to a free and democratic people, and

Desiring to associate the Federal Republic of Germany on a footing of equality with their efforts for peace and security,

The governments of France, the United Kingdom, the United States of America desire to end the occupation regime as soon as possible.

The fulfillment of this policy calls for the settlement of problems of detail in order to liquidate the past and to prepare for the future, and requires the completion of appropriate parliamentary procedures.

In the meantime, the three governments are instructing their High Commissioners to act forthwith in accordance with the spirit of the above policy. In particular, the High Commissioners will not use the powers which are to be relinquished, unless in agreement with the Federal Government, except in the fields of disarmament and demilitarization and in cases where the Federal Government has not been able for legal reasons to take the action or assume the obligations contemplated in the agreed arrangement.

The Brussels Treaty [see "Toward European Union," in this section, above—Ed.] will be strengthened and extended to make it a more effective focus of European integration.

For this purpose the following arrangements have been agreed upon:

(A) The German Federal Republic and Italy will be invited to accede to the treaty, suitably modified to emphasize the objective of European unity, and they have declared themselves ready to do so. The system of mutual automatic assistance in case of attack will thus be extended to the German Federal Republic and Italy.

(B) The structure of the Brussels Treaty will be reinforced. In particular, the Consultative Council provided in the treaty will become a council with powers of decision.

(C) The activities of the Brussels Treaty Organization will be extended to include further important tasks as follows:

The size and general characteristics of the German defense contribution will conform to the contribution fixed for EDC [the European Defense Community].

The maximum defense contribution to NATO of all members of the Brussels Treaty Organization will be determined by a special agreement fixing levels which can only be increased by unanimous consent.

The strength and armaments of the internal defense forces and the police on the Continent of the countries members of the Brussels Treaty Organization will be fixed by agreements within that organization, having regard to their proper function and to existing levels and needs.

LATEST GOAL: A COMMON
WEST EUROPEAN MARKET [8]

On October 31, 1949, Paul G. Hoffman, then head of the Marshall Plan Administration, preached in Paris a kind of sermon on the "integration of the Western European economy." This idea, though not this term,

[8] From "Strength in Unity Sought by Europe," by Harold Callender, chief of the New York *Times* Paris bureau. New York *Times*. p F 1. January 20, 1957. Reprinted by permission.

appeared in the foreign assistance act of 1948 creating the Marshall Plan. Mr. Hoffman went further and urged Europe to form a single market free of tariff barriers.

The sermon was preached to foreign and finance ministers representing the seventeen nations receiving dollar aid for their recovery. It was not taken very seriously except as a possible goal for a remote and somewhat theoretical future. Nobody thought Europe was going to "integrate" very soon, even to please the United States, then the principal sponsor of such unification.

Today this "integration" into a single or "common" market is taken seriously by the most skeptical economists and politicians. A treaty to give it effect may be signed this spring [1957] and ratified soon afterward.

It is now expected the treaty will provide for cutting tariffs 30 per cent in four years and eliminating them in twelve to seventeen years. The common market thus established would include France, West Germany, Italy, Belgium, the Netherlands and Luxembourg. Allied with it in a wider zone of limited free trade and partial "integration" might be Britain, which has hitherto resisted appeals to participate.

What brought about the change in attitude was not the preaching of the United States, which was not lacking in the years following Mr. Hoffman's speech. Nor was it mainly the similar preaching of Jean Monnet, outstanding apostle of what he calls "a United States of Europe" and chief creator of the first real integration, the European Coal and Steel Community.

Europe's change of mind, not yet complete, is attributable principally to a growing realization that in a new world dominated by the United States and the Soviet Union, the nations of Europe, even the former great powers, are relatively small both as economic units and as instruments of political or military power.

This realization reached a kind of climax when Britain and France, having invaded Egypt in November, found it necessary or desirable to yield at once to pressure from the United States and the Soviet Union to stop fighting. [See Section III, North Africa and the Suez Crisis—Ed.]

The economic crisis that followed did nothing to counteract the impression that the European nations should unite in quest of greater strength especially in a time when the loss of colonies had already entailed and might further entail loss of traditional economic assets.

The economic crisis caused by the Suez affair proved more convincing than that during which Mr. Hoffman had spoken.

COMMON MARKET PLAN
WINS INITIAL APPROVAL [9]

Premier Guy Mollet [has] won . . . a conditional and preliminary victory in his effort to take France into a tariff-free common market with five other Western European states. The National Assembly, after a week of debate, approved by 322 votes to 207 a resolution authorizing the Government to complete negotiations for the common market plan with West Germany, Italy, Belgium, the Netherlands and Luxembourg.

The resolution was presented by Premier Mollet's own Socialist party and endorsed by all of the deputies who represent France in the Strasbourg Assembly of Europe. It won the votes of the Socialists, Popular Republicans, dissident Radicals and most of the independents.

[9] From "Mollet Wins Vote in Move for Common Market Pact," by Robert C. Doty, correspondent for the New York *Times*. New York *Times*. p 1+. January 23, 1957. Reprinted by permission.

In opposition were the Communists, who condemned the market as a trap leading to German hegemony over Europe; the Poujadists, who fight any tampering with France's economy; and the Radical followers of former Premier Pierre Mendès-France. M. Mendès-France based his opposition on the ground that France should take national action to put her economy in healthy condition before risking free competition.

The six states, already linked in a supranational Coal and Steel Community, propose to eliminate all tariff and other trade barriers among them by gradual steps over a period of twelve to seventeen years. Concurrently, their negotiators at Brussels are putting the finishing touches on another treaty that, if ratified, would establish an atomic energy community, Euratom, for development in common of nuclear power for peaceful purposes. . . .

In a final plea for approval of the plan, regarded as the keystone for construction of a united Europe, Premier Mollet contended that such action was the only way to make of Europe a world force capable of exercising "independent" influence in international affairs.

"How often between an America sometimes too impulsive, sometimes too slow to understand perils and a disquieting and often menacing Soviet Union, we have wished for the existence of a united Europe, become a world force, not neutral but independent?" he asked.

M. Mollet's speech and the final resolution for the guidance of French negotiators both gave satisfaction to French concern over the impact of free competition on France's high-cost industry, her agriculture and her overseas territories.

Approval of the resolution by the Assembly constitutes no guarantee that the same deputies will vote the same way when they are presented with a treaty spelling out the common market sometime next spring. Most observers were convinced, on the contrary, that the treaty would face very stiff opposition once highly protected French industrial and agricultural interests were in a position to assess from the treaty's details the menaces presented to them by the gradual lowering of barriers to free competition.

To protect French agriculture from loss of domestic and foreign markets, the resolution urged the government to proceed with its plan to seek minimum price levels for foodstuffs within the common market. This would constitute, in effect, a continuation of protection. At the same time, the government was directed to seek long-term contracts embodying price minimums.

It was noted that even the degree of inclusion of agricultural products in the common market envisaged in the French resolution was more than would be acceptable to Britain in negotiations for a larger free-trade zone.

The Assembly voted also to pursue negotiations for association with Britain and possibly other states with guarantees of essential French interests equivalent to those to be contained in the common market treaty.

III. NORTH AFRICA AND
THE SUEZ CRISIS

EDITOR'S INTRODUCTION

The crisis the French have been facing in North Africa should not be viewed simply as another manifestation of the postwar disintegration of the French colonial empire. For one thing, it is part and parcel of the general flare-up of Arab nationalism in the Middle East. (See *The Middle East in the Cold War,* edited by Grant S. McClellan, The Reference Shelf, Volume 28, Number 6, 1956.) Nor can it be seen apart from the present world-wide pattern of resurgent nationalism, both among former colonial peoples and elsewhere. Thus, this section is concerned with French North Africa not just as a French problem but in the larger context of the power struggle in the Middle East.

It bears pointing out that one ramification of the North African problem in recent months has been the French role in the Suez crisis. A manifest aim of French policy at the time was to cause the downfall of President Nasser of Egypt, who has openly encouraged Arab nationalism in French North Africa, but the net effect of the episode was to strengthen his position. At any rate that appeared to be the situation at the end of 1956.

This section opens with an over-all view of French North Africa, its history and character. A leading French commentator, Raymond Aron, presents two major French arguments in answer to the common American view that the French presence in North Africa is an example of old-fashioned colonialism. The article by Herbert Luethy discusses the driving forces of French colonial policy, analyzes its inherent weaknesses, and points out why and where it has failed. An article by a Syrian representative at the United Nations provides a highly critical view of the French role in North Africa. Since no discussion of the North African question would be complete without referring to the solutions proposed by Mendès-France, an article written at the time he was premier reports on his efforts to achieve peaceful and just settlements in Tunisia and Algeria. The attempts at democratization currently being made by the newly independent governments of Tunisia and Morocco are outlined in an article by Benjamin Rivlin. Colin Legum, African correspondent of the London *Observer,* discusses the powerful hold of the *colons* (colonists of French extraction) in Algeria and their disproportionate political influence. Next, the strategic importance of North Africa to Western defense is evaluated. The Suez question is first raised in its relationship to France's position in North Africa. A summary of events leading up to the Middle East crisis is included to orient the reader. An article by James Reston describes the sharp reaction in official Washington to the Anglo-French intervention in Suez. The section closes with an analysis of the problems left in the wake of the Suez expedition.

FRENCH NORTH AFRICA [1]

French North Africa is that part of the French overseas empire which stretches from the Mediterranean to the Atlantic across the northwestern corner of the African continent.

[1] From "North Africa Perils Western Defense," by Sam Stavisky, writer on French and North African affairs for *Nation's Business. Nation's Business.* 43:54-8+. November 1955. Reprinted by permission.

Roughly five times larger than mainland France, the Maghreb ("land of the setting sun") is comprised of Algeria, which has been made an integral part of France, and two flanking protectorates, Morocco, on the west, and Tunisia, on the east.

Although physically a part of the so-called Black Continent, French North Africa (along with Spanish Morocco) has throughout the ages been cut off from the rest of Africa by the Atlas Mountains and the Sahara Desert. Since antiquity, the history of the Maghreb has been influenced by incursions—and cultures—emanating from Europe and the Near East.

The native stock of French North Africa—unlike the indigenous people below the Sahara—is white. The nomadic Berbers, of unknown origin, inhabited the Maghreb from earliest times.

Beginning about 800 B.C., the Berbers were successively forced under the rule of the Phoenicians (who founded Carthage on the Tunisian coast), the Romans (who sacked Carthage in the Punic wars), the Vandals (who overran Rome), and, in the seventh century A.D., the Arabs. Unlike the earlier conquerors, the Arabs remained and imposed both their Moslem religion and culture on the Berbers.

Israelites settled in the Maghreb during the pre-Christian era; others found refuge there after being driven out of Spain, along with the Moors, in the fifteenth century. The French first began to move into the Maghreb in the first half of the nineteenth century.

The population of French North Africa today is about 21 million, or just about half the population of mainland France. The Frenchmen number approximately 1.5 million; Jews, 500,000. The remainder are Berbers, Arabs, or a mixture of both.

How Did France Get There?

After having lost its principal possessions in North America, France, during the early 1800's, was eager to rebuild her overseas empire to keep pace with the expansion of the other European powers, especially England.

During the 1820's, while France was bickering with the Bey of Algiers, a notorious backer of Mediterranean pirates, the Bourbon king, Charles X—whose throne was tottering from internal pressures—converted the quarrel into war. Algiers fell to the French in 1830. It then took the French eighteen years, at a cost of 150,000 French lives and vast financial outlay, to subdue the individual chieftains. In 1871, Algeria was made into an integral part of France.

Although France got its trade-foot into the door of Tunisia in 1830, it was not until 1881 that the Bey formally accepted the protection of the French government. Tunisia was technically a tributary of the disintegrating Ottoman empire, but after the Russians defeated the Turks, and the continental powers met at the Congress of Berlin to divide the spoils, the French got the go-ahead on Tunisia from both England and Germany.

Beginning in 1905, France began a series of deals aimed at attaining control over Morocco. France quietly agreed to give England a free hand in Egypt; Spain, a free hand in northern Morocco; Italy, a free hand in Libya. In return, France was to get a free hand in Morocco. But Emperor William II of Germany balked. As a result, in 1906, twelve Western powers—including the United States—signed an agreement reaffirming the independence of the sultan, but giving France and Spain special police powers there. A few years later, France bought off Germany, ceding 100,000 square miles of holdings in French Equatorial Africa for assent to move into Morocco. The sultan yielded to the "protection" in 1912. . . .

Who Is Fighting Whom?

Although the French governments have, over the years, had to repress or otherwise deal with Arab-Berber revolts and uprisings the fighting today is no simple case of French ruler versus subject. A dual civil war is going on, with extremists in both the French and native populations of North Africa assassinating the moderates who dare speak up for negotiations in place of all-out war.

Currently, quiet reigns in Tunisia, where the Neo-Destour Party, moderate nationalists, maintains leadership after having obtained home rule concessions during the past few months from the French government. ["Destour" means "constitution" in Arabic.—Ed.]

France's recent troubles have occurred in Algeria and French Morocco, where a series of incidents over the past two years culminated . . . [in] August [1955] in the massacre of fifty-one French settlers at Oued Zem by fanatically whipped-up Berber tribesmen.

The events leading to this massacre began two years ago, when the French colonial extremists, headed by Marshal Juin, together with their principal ally, Thami el Glaoui, Berber pasha of Marrakesh, forced the removal of Sultan Sidi Mohammed ben Youssef. Since his accession to the throne in 1927, the sultan had collaborated with the French but, about three years ago, under pressure of the native nationalist movement, he had become increasingly uncooperative. The French government was opposed to the change, but was too deeply involved in a general public service strike at home to care much about the sultanate. A more pliable puppet,

Sidi Mohammed ben Moulay Arafa, was installed as Sultan of Morocco.

This act gave the Istiqlal, the leading native national group, an unexpected boost. Although the old sultan never had been popular before, his return to the throne —from exile to Madagascar—became the rallying cry of the nationalists. The opponents and supporters of the new sultan became increasingly terroristic in their activities against each other, and against moderates within their own ranks. Tension mounted. Incidents increased. . . .

In an effort to find some easing of the tension, French Premier Faure sent Gilbert Grandval, who had earned a reputation as a tough but able administrator in the Saar, as resident-general to Morocco. He investigated, and urged that the puppet be deposed, an interim regency be set up, and negotiations opened with the native nationalists. He urged speed, action before August 20 [1955], the date marking the second anniversary of the switch in sultans.

The French colonial extremists and the Berber chief, el Glaoui, opposed this solution. So did the conservative political bloc in France. Premier Faure, himself a moderate, delayed action and it was not until after August 20—and the massacre at Oued Zem—that he forced his coalition cabinet to accept the principle of the Grandval plan—meanwhile, removing Grandval as resident-general of Morocco in way of propitiation.

Caught between the irreconcilable pressures demanding concession and repression, both in France and Morocco, the Faure government teetered for weeks in a state of near collapse, while members of the Faure cabinet, along with top level military and political officials, sabotaged the Faure move toward giving some home rule to Morocco.

Meanwhile, already-divided France became deeply embroiled in a new crisis over Algeria. The Moroccan outburst revived old fires of nationalism in Algeria, which for more than one hundred years had been integrated as part of France. The French have been particularly proud of their development of Algeria, of making it a part of France, of giving Algerians the right to French citizenship. But even the so-called assimilated Algerians suddenly have publicly opposed integration, demanding autonomy if not actual independence.

This move was given further impetus when the United Nations General Assembly unexpectedly voted to take up the Algerian issue over French protest that the issue was a strictly domestic one. However, the anticolonial Asian-Arab bloc, backed by Russia and her satellites, voted out the issue against the opposition of the United States and Great Britain. Outraged, France walked out of the UN Assembly.

The French defeat in the UN encouraged new outbreaks in both Algeria and Morocco, further complicating the situation.

Although the basic cause of the troubles in North Africa is the quest of the native peoples for home rule and independence, there is little doubt the Communists have been helping the nationalists with funds and otherwise through the small Communist parties in North Africa and the big Communist party within France proper.

The North African Liberation Committee, a group seeking independence for all of North Africa, has been propagandizing the Maghreb via radio from Egypt and Syria. The Arab League has been similarly fostering discontent. Both groups are suspected of being financed in part by the Communists. . . .

The Communists, as a matter of Moscow-directed policy, have generally been making a fetish of anti-colonialism and pro-Arabism. Additionally, it has been Moscow's policy to seek to weaken the North Atlantic Treaty Organization. Unrest in French Morocco forces France to move troops from the European to the African continent, thereby weakening NATO defenses.

In addition to Communist aid, however, the nationalists in North Africa are believed to be getting both encouragement and assistance from naturally sympathetic fellow Moslem countries.

Why Doesn't France Get Out?

France couldn't get out of North Africa easily, even if she wished.

Algeria is, from the official French point of view, as integral a part of France as New Mexico is a part of the United States. Right now, at least, most Frenchmen would consider giving Algeria back to the native Arab-Berber population unthinkable. Algerians are citizens of France. (The representation of the native Algerians in the French Parliament, however, is restricted, so that the nationalists charge that Algerians are second-class citizens.)

While Morocco and Tunisia are technically protectorates of France, they have, in effect, been colonies, and have long been considered the gems of France's colonial crown. No French government politically could grant complete independence to Morocco and Tunisia, and abandon the French colonials to Moslem rule. . . .

France has spent billions of dollars and tens of thousands of lives subduing North Africa, colonizing and developing the area, and has been especially proud of her efforts in improving the education, health, and economic standards of the native peoples.

Even today, as in the past, many Frenchmen see in their North African overseas territory—which possesses excellent land for farming and weather conditions akin to those of southern California—a natural outlet for growing home population.

Strategically, control of North Africa increases France's position in the Mediterranean and provides a vital source of military manpower.

Economically, North Africa is an important source of raw materials for France's industries.

THE "FRENCH PRESENCE" IN NORTH AFRICA [2]

There is no subject on which French and American opinion splits so sharply as on that of colonies in general and North Africa in particular.

From the American point of view, the French presence in North Africa is an example of colonialism, therefore deplorable and fit to be damned. And the Frenchman, meeting this summary damnation, has a tendency to answer that colonialism would have existed in America had the Indian population been encouraged instead of blighted by contact with the white invaders.

Let us drop these sterile arguments and try to understand the two major arguments of French opinion.

The first is that, almost unanimously—left and right, conservative and fellow traveler—French opinion does not admit that it has anything to be ashamed of in North Africa. Items:

Tunisia had 1.5 million inhabitants in 1881; it has 3.5 million today.

[2] By Raymond Aron, chief columnist for the French paper *Le Figaro*. *Time*. 66:20-1. July 4, 1955. Reprinted by permission from *Time* magazine, July 4, 1955. Courtesy Time Inc.

In Algeria, the population increased from about 2.5 million a century ago to about 9.5 million today.

Except for Lebanon (which twelve years ago was a French mandate), "colonized" Tunisia has a higher density of paved roads and highways than any Arab country in the Middle East, more telephones per inhabitant, probably more hospital beds.

The second French argument is that any oversimplified solution, any sudden and total "liberation," would not resolve the immense problems of North Africa. The departure of the French would inevitably precipitate chaos. The French minority of North Africa—1 million in Algeria, 270,000 in Tunisia, 360,000 in Morocco—have contributed a share in the economic and cultural development of the country which is disproportionate to their numbers. In general, farming methods are more modern and profits are higher on lands cultivated by French *colons*. Emigration of Frenchmen might precipitate the collapse of the country's resources at a moment when the pressure of growing population is particularly strong; the handing over of all power to an improvised government might touch off an emigration which everyone wishes to avoid.

Beyond these arguments, which are self-evident to French eyes, there are the criticisms of what the French have failed to accomplish, and disagreements on measures which must be taken.

In North Africa, as in most underdeveloped countries, the increase in population has outstripped that of natural resources, because medical progress has moved faster than economic progress. The birth rate has not increased, but the death rate has diminished. France has never stopped investing heavily in North Africa, especially since the war. In Algeria, the first four-year equipment plan represented a total of $728 million; the second foresees an expenditure of $820 million. But during the first plan, it is estimated that the population increased by 9 per cent and production by 10 per cent. The standard of living, therefore, remained approximately the same.

To assure a higher standard of living, we must spend at least $285 million more. Continental France finances about three fourths of this special budget. For the whole of Africa, investment expenditures now approach the neighborhood of $570 million. They should be increased by about 50 per cent to 100 per cent in order to ensure a rise in the standard of living.

The population pressure is not the only cause of political conflicts, but it inevitably aggravates the conflicts which colonialism creates all by itself, even in a successful union. The French minority—*colons*, civil servants, shopkeepers, industrialists—are privileged in comparison to the mass of the native population. The revolt of the masses against the privileged classes, inevitable in all underdeveloped countries, is often directed against colonizers and takes a nationalist accent.

So do the aspirations of the cultivated minorities, hesitating between their traditional Moslem culture and religion on one hand, and the Western culture brought by France on the other. Their nationalistic feelings are increased, exacerbated, when their young university graduates have trouble finding work suited to their talents, and, as a consequence, feel that they have been exiled from their native land. There are too many places filled by Frenchmen in the Tunisian and Moroccan bureaucracies which could be filled by natives.

But opening wide the doors of administration to North African youth would not be enough to satisfy nationalist aspirations. The crux of the question is to find out if these aspirations can be satisfied progressively in friendly collaboration with the French, or satisfied only in conflict with them. The conviction of the majority of French opinion is that this progressive transformation is possible. And the example of Tunisia bears witness to this.

Tunisia

The French were divided into two schools on this subject. Some thought that cooperation could be organized within the framework with a Franco-Tunisian government. Others thought that we must grant the moderate nationalists internal autonomy, and fix, by a negotiated agreement, the rights and duties of the Tunisian state and the French minority, thus allowing a new form of Franco-Tunisian community to develop naturally. This second school has carried the day. Negotiations, in which Mendès-France took the lead, have resulted in the signature of conventions which we hope will soon be ratified. Returning in triumph to his own country, Habib Bourguiba of Tunisia spoke of the independence of Tunisia but also of the interdependence of Tunisia and of France. So we find that a nationalist, steeped in French culture, has formulated the ruling thesis of French opinion.

Morocco

The example of Tunisia will have repercussions in the rest of North Africa, especially Morocco. At the present moment, Franco-Moroccan discussions have been interrupted by the dynastic question. The replacement of the old Sultan, who was both a civil and religious leader, has offended an important section of Moroccan opinion which has never recognized the new Sultan. The terrorism which has been launched against Frenchmen and against Moroccans who are reputedly pro-French, and the counter-terrorism which has struck down

Moroccans as well as Frenchmen who are reputedly favorable to certain reforms, have created a tragic situation. Reasonable opinion in France does not misunderstand the dangers of this breakdown, but it remains convinced, and rightly, it seems to me, that a chance still remains for a Moroccan evolution akin to the Tunisian evolution. [Since this article was written, Morocco has been granted autonomy and Sidi Mohammed ben Youssef reinstated as Sultan.—Ed.]

When the French arrived in Tunisia at the end of the nineteenth century, and in Morocco at the beginning of the twentieth, neither the Bey of Tunis nor the Sultan of Morocco exercised effective authority over the whole of his kingdom. Their authority ceased some distance from the cities. The colonial power has revived, rebuilt, reinforced the authority of the Tunisian and Moroccan state. These states are today made of bits and pieces, of traditional elements and of Western institutions brought by the French. Tomorrow, Tunisians and Moroccans can be the heirs of a state which the French have brought to life.

Algeria

Another more difficult situation exists in Algeria, where there is no Algerian state (as there was barely a trace of one, more than a century ago, when the French arrived). Algeria is composed of French departments, in many ways assimilated into those of continental France. For a long time there was a school of French opinion which favored assimilation pure and simple. One scarcely thinks this to be possible today. The Islamic religion is too big a barrier between Algerians and Frenchmen, the standard of living is too unequal on either side of the Mediterranean, the cost of investments which would be needed to raise Algeria to the level of the home country is too much beyond the means of France. To obtain results comparable to what has been achieved in Tunisia, some beginning will have to be made toward the creation of a Franco-Algerian state, linked to France.

These are the facts, these are the ideas, which I think the majority of French opinion holds. I have omitted an important factor: the propaganda coming from Arab countries, and the organization, encouraged and subsidized by them, which aims at creating and extending a zone of guerrilla warfare. In Algeria the guerrilla warfare in the Aurès Mountains and the terrorism in Constantine have local causes, but they would not spread without outside help. These deplorable events encourage the worst partisans on both sides, those who accept no change and those who rely on violence. Hit-and-run warfare paves the way, not for "liberation" but for chaos.

American opinion, American government, by their words and by their silence, by their deeds and by their abstentions, are making a fateful intervention. It is for them to decide if they want to encourage the extension of disorder in regions vital for the defense of the West, or to help Frenchmen, Algerians, Tunisians and Moroccans to prove, by their peaceful cooperation, that Western civilization protects its own treasures, and that the friendship of Christians and Moslems is possible.

THE CRISIS OF FRENCH COLONIALISM [3]

To speak today of the French Colonial Empire is, of course, to speak of something belonging to the past. Juridically speaking, the Empire no longer exists, for the

[3] From article by Herbert Luethy, Swiss political analyst and author of "France Against Herself." *Atlantic Monthly.* 197:60-5. May 1956. Reprinted by permission.

French Constitution of 1946 replaced it by the vague and never clearly defined concept of the French Union, which in theory at least excludes all idea of domination. For years the politicians of France acted as though they could change the name from Empire to Union without having to alter anything else, but that illusion has since been cruelly shattered. While the French possessions in Asia—the most peripheral of the Empire—have had to be abandoned, the African mass of the old Empire so far remains intact. But it is already clear that if any of it is to be saved, it will have to be through far-reaching changes in France's relations with her overseas territories.

To understand what it is that is now in the process of changing, we must first have some idea of what the Empire once was. To find the living incarnation of the French imperial idea you have to go down to Negro Africa and meet the dark-skinned voter of Senegal who proclaims his French citizenship with exactly the same pride that Saint Paul took in calling himself a *civis romanus*—with the consciousness that this is the supreme dignity that man can aspire to. Indeed, in certain of its fundamental aspects this French Empire has no other parallel in history than the Roman—above all in its conception of universal civilization in the proper and primitive sense of the word: that in which to "civilize" means to "make citizens." And yet the France of the Third Republic which built this Empire bore little resemblance, either in power or in will power, to Rome, mistress of the ancient world. The French Empire, indeed, has been one of the most paradoxical and misunderstood realizations in European history; and like many other historic achievements, we may only be able to do it full justice in retrospect, when we can compare what follows with what went before.

Even in France, people began taking notice of this immense imperial domain only when the emancipated countries of Asia and the Middle East started attacking it from all sides. The truth is that the colonies and metropolitan France have not shared the same past, and it is probably since the Liberation of 1944 that they have definitely ceased to understand each other. It was with deep instinctive distrust that the "internal" resistance saw troops and leaders from the colonies arrive in France in the days of liberation. It was the meeting of two forces which were strangers and slightly suspicious of each other. Liberated France hastened—on paper at any rate—to abolish its Colonial Empire. As usual, it was only the name that was being abolished. But this embarrassed haste was characteristic. To talk of the Colonial Empire in the Third Republic had always been to talk of something scandalous. It was something which existed and which Frenchmen could take pride in, but basically it was contrary to republican principles. . . .

Today the work of French colonization enjoys less popular esteem than ever at home. To judge by the Paris press, the war in Indo-China was one uninterrupted series of sordid deals, odious traffickings, and peculations, from the "Emperor of the Night Clubs," Bao Dai, to the constantly half-smothered and rekindled scandals involving piasters, peddlers of political influence, and lucrative acts of treason. Recent events in North Africa have likewise brought out the sullen hostility existing between the parliamentary republic at home and the overseas French—settlers, high administrative officials, and officers of the Army of Africa—who have consistently refused to respect the decisions of the "government in Paris." The Moroccan coup d'état of August 1953, which removed Sultan Ben Youssef from his throne, was a local plot in the purest Franco style engineered by Marshal Juin and the Pasha of Marrakesh against the vacillating will of the French government.

Yet it would be equally possible to write another history of overseas France in which the quarrels and scandals in Europe appear only as stupid and sometimes destructive interruptions of the vast, audacious, patient, century-long work of those pioneers and Empire-builders whose achievements ignorant politicians and demagogues at home have never ceased to dissipate on the Rhine and in Flanders, if not in budgetary debates and corridor intrigues. For France has certainly the greatest and oldest colonial tradition of all the nations of Europe. Prior to the English, the French between 1650 and 1750 established a protectorate over a large part of India, the last five trading posts of which were surrendered to New Delhi a year and a half ago. They were the first to bring European colonization to the interior of North America. France is the only country which, having lost almost all of one vast Colonial Empire, set out again to build another—one that is still the second largest in the world.

The Empire of Richelieu and Colbert, however, was not the first; the history of French colonialism really starts at the beginning of our millennium with the Norman expeditions and reaches its apogee in the Crusades and the Franco-Latin Empire of the East. Barely one hundred years after their debarkation on the soil of France, those Scandinavian pirates, the Normans, took off again as French conquerors, sowing French culture and language in every direction, from England to Sicily and Jerusalem. Here for the first time we encounter that astonishing power of assimilation of a people which —right up to yesterday—had no doubt of its ability to weld all peoples and races together in the melting pot of France, and to turn them into Frenchmen whether they were Kabyles, Tuaregs, Madagascans, Annamites, or Indians.

Underlying this "absurd dream" is the naive and un-limited confidence in its own human and spiritual inde-structibility of a nation which has always wished to possess not an ethnic or racial but a cultural unity, open to everything that is human. Since the Middle Ages there has existed what we might call a French "cultural imperialism" which, alongside of other more down-to-earth motives, has been one of the driving forces of French colonial, and even foreign, policy. This cultural imperialism of France has always implied a degree of receptivity to, and a readiness to appropriate, what is foreign. . . .

The paradoxical feature of this Empire has been its idealism. The Empire of France has always been a luxury, a question of prestige, of international rank, of cultural glory, far more than something necessary or useful. Tending to be self-sufficient, metropolitan France has never felt the desire or the need to exploit the work of her Empire-builders. Thus, never even in the most limited sense has she developed an imperial economy. Before the First World War, when she was the banker of the world, France invested 45 million francs abroad, but of this immense sum barely one tenth went to her colonies. . . . The military conquest and pacification of the colonies cost it 10 billion francs, but it could not even spare half that amount for their economic develop-ment. In the last budget for the colonies before the Second World War—that of 1938—the French state devoted 2.5 per cent of its allocations to its overseas possessions, four fifths of which went to the army.

Behind the tariff walls shielding the colonies, French trading companies have lived comfortably off the sale of commercial products manufactured for the natives and off the import of colonial products sold on the home market. From the start it was extensive colonization of the mercantile and almost feudal type, with trading stations and large landed estates rather than small settlements and industrial plants. The colonies have thus become simple extensions rather than partners of the metropolitan French economy.

The economy of Algeria after one century of French domination offers the most dramatic illustration of this tendency carried to extremes. With fierce exclusiveness the French settlers of Algeria grow wheat, the overproduction of which in France has already entailed a cutback in sown areas; and they produce wine, which, since the drinking of alcohol is forbidden to faithful Moslems by the Koran, can only find a market in France, a wine-producing country par excellence. The result is that metropolitan France must now protect herself with a tariff barrier against this very Algeria which is integrated into the political, administrative, and fiscal system of the "one and indivisible" Republic.

This, of course, is an extreme case. Yet it is a fact that up until the First World War nine tenths of what France—herself an agricultural country—imported from her colonies consisted of foodstuffs. The progress made by the banana-growers of French West Africa has caused panic among French fruit-growers at home; coconut-palm and ground-nut oils have seriously threatened French olive oil; rum from Martinique has competed with French cognac and *eau de vie*. As a result, hardly a single colonial product has been spared by the French customs. Prohibited too has been all industrial development in the colonies, even of the humblest local industries for the processing of native foodstuffs or minerals. The sanctity of metropolitan France's monopoly position was always the first principle of French colonialism.

Two territories, before the war, stood out as exceptions in this scheme of things: the two youngest and most modern of France's colonies, Morocco and Indo-

China. A more up-to-date brand of colonization was able to assert itself here—thanks, in the case of Indo-China, to its very distance from France, which in a way protected it; and, in the case of Morocco, to the grandiose views of Marshal Lyautey, who "launched" the protectorate much as one launches a business. In the latter case, this has been furthered by the fact that the Treaty of Algeciras of 1906 recognized the commercial "open door" and thus prevented Morocco's incorporation into the French colonial system. Here the spirit of French enterprise has shown that when faced with foreign competition it can meet the test, and that all it has lacked elsewhere has been the invigorating experience of being obliged to stand up to its rivals.

One Hundred Million Citizens

What metropolitan France has always expected of "greater France" is the "making of Frenchmen"— French citizens, of course, but first and foremost French soldiers. For the native élites the narrow gate providing access to French citizenship has always been the French high school diploma; but the great highway open to all has been the chance of serving under French colors in time of war.

All the French "laws of assimilation" and the mass grants of citizenship date from war years: 1870-1871, 1914-1918, 1943-1945. It seems to have been General Mangin, that hero of the First World War, who first spoke of France as a country numbering not 40 but 100 million Frenchmen. It is on the battlefield that the great dream of making men of all races into sons of France has found its basic and concrete expression. In her colonies France has found no dearth of soldiers. Here, where it has kept the spirit of the *ancien régime* alive

more successfully than at home, the army has been the
great crucible of assimilation. Out of Arabs and Berbers,
out of Senegalese and Madagascans, it has created French
patriots; whereas only too often French schools have
produced intellectuals who, in the sacred name of republican principles, have revolted against French colonial
rule. Nothing could better illustrate the efficacy of the
military crucible than that corps which groups under its
banners men who are neither French subjects nor the
sons of primitive peoples—the Foreign Legion.

Here again the Second World War dealt a mortal
blow to the old French imperial structure, not so much
by the defeats that France suffered in the course of it in
Europe and Asia as by the chaotic events of its aftermath.
For the old French colonial army, with all its glamour
and glory, is now no more than a memory of yesterday.
At the end of the war the Army of Africa was simply
liquidated for having been an "instrument of Vichy." . . .

It is true, of course, that of these 100 million Frenchmen, 60 million remain far from the appointed goal and
only too often very distant indeed from what may be
called human dignity. But in this myth they are on the
march, and the elect, who have already reached the goal,
beckon them on. In the symbolic figure of the Negro
governor of the Tchad, Eboué, the first Frenchman in
Africa to rally to General de Gaulle in 1940, this myth
received its first great embodiment.

The first imperial conference, held by the Free French
in January of 1944 under de Gaulle's chairmanship, re-
affirmed the principles and aims of French colonialism
more categorically than ever.

We read from time to time [declared the Commissioner
for the Colonies, René Pleven] that this war must end by
what is called the emancipation of colonial peoples. But in
the great Colonial France there are neither peoples to be

freed nor racial discriminations to be abolished. . . . There are populations that we intend to lead step by step to higher stages of individual expression, and in the highest stages to full political franchise, but which have no wish to experience any form of independence other than the French. . . .

When the time came in 1945 to transform the French Empire into the French Union, the idea of granting the Arabs of North Africa, the Madagascans, or the peoples of the ancient civilization of Indo-China the vital minimum of autonomy which the British Commonwealth, if only for reasons of administrative efficiency, grants to the humblest Negro kingdom proved even more inadmissible for the French colonial reformer of the Left than for the most impenitent colonialist of the Right. . . .

When the first Constitutional Convention reassembled in Paris after the war, it solemnly condemned colonialism and treated the institutions of the French Union as a simple chapter of the Constitution of the Republic. "The Colonial Empire is dead," proclaimed Pierre Cot, the head of the Convention's Committee on Colonial Problems. "In its place we are setting up the French Union. Enriched, ennobled, and enlarged, France tomorrow will number 100 million citizens and free men." Unanimously adopted by the Convention, this . . . [law] of May 7, 1945, has remained the charter of French colonial policy ever since: "From the 1st of June 1946, all natives of overseas territories (Algeria included) are legally considered citizens, on the same footing with the nationals of metropolitan France."

Thus the nation of 100 million citizens became a political reality. . . . It is difficult to go back on pledges, no matter how lightly made, once they have received the solemn consecration of law. To limit the damage, the second French Constitutional Convention, held in 1946, contented itself with leaving every possible escape hatch open for future "interpretive decrees" and local statutes. Thus revised, the Constitution of the French Union was no more than a hodgepodge of contradictory articles and conflicting theses. At the very end a couple of laconic paragraphs were thrown in which allowed everything to tumble back into the old well-worn groove. The French parliament remained the legislator for overseas France; the governor of each colony, named by the French government and responsible to it alone, remained the head of the local administration and the sole depository of executive power. Behind the smoke-screen promise of assimilation for all the peoples of the French Union there remained the stubborn realities of administrative centralization—the wordless fact of colonialism in practice.

The Tragedy of Algeria

All this engendered an inevitable crisis for the new French Union. It was first felt over the problems raised by the concept of assimilation, and notably in the case of Algeria, an integral part of metropolitan France. When for the first time in 1946 thirteen Algerian Moslems, elected by a separate and less-privileged electoral college, took up their seats in the French Assembly, it came as a shock to the French to realize that these men felt themselves more Algerian and Arab than French. The result was a clash, at once tragic and grotesque, between the stirring old notion of human progress and this jarring new reality. "I am here to represent the interests of my country," declared Ferhat Abbas, the leader of the autonomous movement that had issued the "Algerian Manifesto." Whereupon he was assailed from all sides by indignant cries: "No, sir, your country is France!" . . .

What in the French Assembly has only too often been a lamentable comedy has become a full-scale tragedy in Algeria. For the sublime ideal of 100 million French citizens, translated into a juridical fiction, has become a deadly trap from which there is no escape. Since legally there are no such things as Algerians (in the parliamentary jargon they are referred to simply as "French Moslems"), there can be no compromise. Their rights may be limited, they may have a standard of living that is ten times lower than the French, four fifths of them may never have gone to school and be unable to read or write a word of French, but according to the official myth they are French citizens. Any Algerian nationalist or autonomist is thus automatically regarded as a bad citizen, a rebel, a traitor, and a deserter, rather than as a partner with whom the ticklish problems of coexistence should be discussed.

It would be a grave mistake to see nothing but hypocrisy in all this, even though there is no lack of administrative hypocrisy in practice. The idea of a "greater France," of France as a melting pot of races and civilizations, has been one of the few genuine empire-building ideas of modern times. It is this myth which once gave the French Empire its cohesion and it is still so deeply rooted in the French consciousness that the crisis affecting it reaches down to its very foundations. It is a crisis in the pretension to universality of a civilization which has always aspired to be that of all mankind. . . .

Within the walls of a single monolithic state—"one and indivisible"—the French melting pot of races has ceased to bubble and has grown cold. The bureaucratic and juridical assimilation of the French colonies has become the very caricature of the true assimilative force which the idea of French civilization once possessed. The unilateral subjection of all citizens of the Empire to a uniform administrative yoke has, in fact, stunted all efforts at mutual comprehension and the exchange of views between Frenchmen and native populations.

The transformation of Algeria into a "100 per cent French land" is an extreme example of the tyranny of this legal fiction. For one thing today is certain: the Algerians are less likely than ever to become French now that they see Tunisia and Morocco on either side of them becoming independent Moslem states. For half a century the French administration of the protectorates of Tunisia and Morocco was—in spite of obvious differences of status—copied from the administration of Algeria, and nothing can now insulate Algeria from a contagious influence working in the reverse direction.

Yet complete secession from the French Union would offer Algeria no future. After one hundred years of colonization and mutual exchanges of populations, the links between France and Algeria have grown so strong that they can no longer be cut without mortally injuring both countries. The hatred that has arisen between Algerians and Frenchmen has, in the last analysis, only become so bitter because it was born of a frustrated love, of disillusioned hopes. The Moslems of North Africa have heeded the voice of Cairo because for so long Paris stubbornly ignored their existence. In this way the three countries of French North Africa have slipped into violence and bloodshed.

Yet all the French had to do, after years of vacillation and mounting terror, was to recognize the autonomy of Tunisia, and overnight the nationalist leaders there began throwing out the agitators from Cairo and proclaiming that they are closer to France and Europe than they are to Cairo and the Arab League. So too the Moslems of Algeria have no wish to change the color of their skins in order to become "assimilated Frenchmen"; but once they are no longer required to undergo this mystic and impossible transubstantiation, they will discover— to their own amazement—that they carry the imprint of France on their hearts and minds.

Thus the present agony of Algeria is basically only one aspect of the general crisis in France's relations with the rest of the world. For ten years France has remained spellbound by the notion of her absolute and indivisible "sovereignty." She has refused to seize her real opportunities, and has clung tenaciously to her empty titles to a glorious past. In reality, the awakened nationalisms of Asia and Africa have never demanded the severing of all links with France; they have required only *home rule,* which unfortunately is rejected wholesale by the French conception of sovereignty. . . .

With more confidence in herself, France could have taken the real—which is to say, the intellectual and human —leadership of these associations among equals. And the problem which thus poses itself for France today, not only in her relations to her colonies but also in her relations to Europe and the world, is this: Can she free herself from the armor of traditional ideologies, institutions, and legal notions which, instead of protecting her living energies, both spiritual and physical, has succeeded in stifling them? Is the French idea of universal civilization capable of being renovated and revitalized by that receptivity to the new and the different which is the indispensable companion of all cultural radiation, or is it doomed to be choked to death by that cultural chauvinism which in recent years has so often raised its head?

AN ARAB VIEW OF THE FRENCH ROLE
IN NORTH AFRICA [4]

The Arab nationalist movement had its birth when the Arab people struggled to free themselves from the yoke of the Ottoman Empire, it continues today in Arab action to throw off the yoke of Western imperialism, whether French, British, or other. The movement is inspired by a common language, common history, and a common set of values and principles which have united the Arab world for hundreds of years and which the present state divisions have not been able to destroy. It would be extremely surprising if the Arabs did not aim at the ultimate unity of the Arab world. . . .

Even before the new Egyptian Constitution was written, the Arab League in cooperation with the Asian-African group brought the question of Tunisia and of Morocco before the United Nations General Assembly, in 1952, at the seventh session. And although France boycotted the Assembly during the consideration of the questions of Tunisia and Morocco, two resolutions were adopted by the General Assembly calling upon France to take measures compatible with the aspirations of the Tunisian and Moroccan people. France ignored these recommendations and, in fact, adopted repressive measures which seriously worsened the already acute situation. The struggle therefore continued, and the liberation movement became stronger than ever.

Very recently, however, France has agreed to revoke the unequal treaties which she had with both Tunisia and Morocco and has declared the complete independence of these two North African countries. We cannot but give

[4] From "The Aspirations of the People of French North Africa," by Muhammad H. El-Farra, Chief of the United Nations Section of the League of Arab States Delegation and attaché of the Permanent Delegation of Syria to the United Nations. *Annals of the American Academy of Political and Social Science.* 306:10-16. July 1956. Reprinted by permission.

France credit for this wise decision. I want to say with all sincerity and frankness, however, that we should have liked to see a decision adopted earlier. A more prompt and liberal recognition of the sovereignty of these North African countries and their nationalist claims would no doubt have averted much bloodshed and bitterness and human suffering.

Now that Tunisia and Morocco are gaining complete independence, I do not deem it necessary to bring before you a detailed picture of the tragic history of these two countries. We prefer to look to the future, since our only desire is to see peace and harmony prevail in North Africa. All that I should like to emphasize at this stage is that this whole movement is one movement. It cannot be divided. It is wrong to call it a Tunisian movement or Moroccan or Algerian or Libyan or Egyptian. It is an Arab liberation movement. Therefore, you cannot call the support given by Egypt or Syria or Iraq or any other Arab country the intervention of a foreign state. It is wrong to call this support "external influence at work trying to undermine the French position throughout North Africa," in the words of the United States Ambassador to France. Such a charge amounts to an intentional denial of history and facts, a denial of the movement of reawakening which had begun earlier in the Arab regions of the Ottoman Empire. Arabs fought hard to emancipate themselves, first from Ottoman rulers and then from those Western powers which inherited Ottoman imperialism. Their war was a revolt against domination and exploitation. They wanted to save the Arab homeland from foreign conquest. They were inspired by common cultural and spiritual values.

These values were among the strong forces which have since the conquest in 1830 defeated all attempts to assimilate and integrate Algeria into France. One hun-

dred and twenty-six years have passed, and this integration continues to be mere fiction. When the Asian-
African group brought the question of Algeria before the
United Nations and the matter was inscribed on the
agenda of the tenth session of the General Assembly, the
main French argument was that Algerians were Frenchmen and that Algeria was an integral part of France.
This argument was not accepted by the United Nations,
who decided by a majority of 28 votes to 27, with 5
abstentions, to inscribe the question of Algeria on the
agenda of the United Nations—a decision which caused
France to withdraw from the United Nations General
Assembly.

Although France was unable to convince the world
that Algeria is France and that Arabs are Frenchmen,
she is still using force and repressive measures to achieve
a goal which she could not achieve during the past 126
years. It is hard, however, to resist the tide of nationalism. No power, no matter how mighty, can hold it back
or slow it down. In spite of 126 years of French teaching
and preaching, the people of Algeria continue to resist
this fiction of integration and assimilation. For 126 years
France has been telling the Algerian Arabs, "You are
Frenchmen," and for 126 years these people have been
answering, "No, we are not, we cannot be; we are Arabs
having our own language and heritage and traditions and
culture." . . .

The 850,000 French settlers in Algeria, composing
less than one tenth of the population, are guaranteed
representation totaling one half of all representatives in
the principal Algerian elected bodies. Algeria has thirty
seats in the French National Assembly, but only half of
the seats are reserved for Moslem deputies and even
these few Moslems are not the true representatives of the
people.

You may be surprised to know that the inhabitants, who are Arabs, are denied the right to learn their own language, Arabic. France refused to teach Arabic in the government schools. Only in a few Islamic schools and in three secondary schools attended by five hundred students are Arabic studies pursued. In the French secondary schools, Arabic is taught as a foreign language. Not only this, but no Algerian is allowed to teach Arabic unless he obtains a certificate that he has mastered the French language.

You may be surprised, also, to know that teaching Algerian history is a crime. In October 1954, one Sheikh Zarrouki was sentenced to four years' imprisonment for teaching Algerian history. This may sound strange but it is a fact. The French believe that teaching Arabic and Algerian history would be an obstacle in the way of integration.

Ever since the invasion the French colonists who exploit the country and enjoy its wealth have done their best to keep the Algerian Arabs illiterate. Today only 50,000 Moslems out of 11 million have grammar school certificates.

In the economic field, Algerians still have to turn to the French market to satisfy their need of manufactured goods and are still exporters of raw material to the advantage of the French business interests.

This may explain why France walked out of the United Nations. She could not face with pride the United Nations and say, "The Algerians, after 126 years of my rule, are enjoying equal citizenship." France could not come before the United Nations and say, "The Algerians have become an inseparable part of France, having everything in common with the French." France has failed to show that Algeria is France and that the Arabs are French. . . .

Your modern Western culture and its values and thoughts have penetrated our lands. They had meaning for us since they are rooted in the same traditions in which our own culture is rooted. Today cultural institutions of the West function all over the Arab world, and with this advance of Western thought, the Arab has had increasing confidence in these values. Therefore it is very disappointing to him to see the West preach one thing and practice something else, to see the knowledge, thought, and ideals which the West advanced with one hand being destroyed by the other. The practice of colonialism and imperialism in North Africa and the Middle East perforce reflects on the authenticity of the ethical values the West preaches. Is it surprising, then, that many an Arab is inclined to reject, with disappointment, the values of Western culture as insincere and false? . . .

Today we have the question of North Africa. The people of Algeria are now extending their hands to France and begging her to find an equitable and just solution to their problem. They are determined to put an end to the policy of French subjugation and exploitation. They are ready to negotiate with France a reasonable and practical treaty provided that France recognizes the fact that assimilation and integration are impossible between two nations which have nothing in common. It is up to France to remember that the time of nineteenth-century colonialism is over; that the policy of divide and rule is no longer workable; that only a new approach to the question of North Africa and all the problems of the Middle East can bring back the prestige of the Western world; that the real interests of the West can be best served by a change in the foreign policy of the Western powers.

The United States, I am sure, can play a leading part in this change. Good will and wise statesmanship on the part of the French government and the United States will still help to avoid bloodshed and decrease tension in the Arab world. The door is still open for understanding and mutual cooperation.

MENDES-FRANCE'S NORTH AFRICAN POLICIES [5]

Shortly after the fall of Dienbienphu, a French Deputy wrote to Premier Joseph Laniel:

At the moment when a succession of errors has made Vietnam a tomb of so many French lives and hopes, a serious new menace is hanging over North Africa, part of the body and soul of France. [We are acting] in Africa as if wholly ignorant of events in the Far East. We are deliberately closing our eyes to the existence of deep national currents . . . among people whom we ourselves have given a taste for liberty. While we are forced now to grant Indo-China everything we once refused Ho Chi Minh and more, our position in North Africa is still one of categorical refusal. We are trying to make up for the weakness of this policy with police violence of the most oppressive, the most odious sort. It isn't necessary to study geopolitics to understand that North Africa is about to become one of the neuralgic points of the globe.

The writer was Pierre Mendès-France, and during his . . . months in office the cumulative tensions of many years . . . brought France to a critical point in its relations with its whole North African empire.

Mendès-France's way of meeting the crisis in Tunisia and Algeria became a matter of bitter debate in Paris. . . .

Premiers in the past have tended to follow the classic rules of colonial administration: Concede nothing to the

[5] From "Bloody Fingers and the Loosening Grip," by Claire Sterling, staff writer for the *Reporter*. *Reporter*. 11:16-20. December 30, 1954. Reprinted by permission.

native population if nothing is happening, and concede nothing if something is happening, because it would be wrong to give in to force. Mendès-France has broken both rules.

Tunisia

He was certainly giving in to force when he flew to Tunis [in 1954] to present his proposal for full internal autonomy to Sidi Mohammed al-Amin Bey, the nominal if powerless sovereign of the Tunisian protectorate. Tunisia was paralyzed by terrorism at the moment of his arrival. The terror had begun in the spring of 1952, when the nationalist Neo-Destour announced its intention of planting a bomb a day until Tunisia was liberated. By the following winter, a counter-terrorist movement had made its appearance, with the assassination of Ferhat Hached, the leader of the largest Tunisian trade union. By the spring of 1954, violence had taken three forms: individual killings in the cities, carried out by the Neo-Destour; raids on French *colons* in the country by bands of Fellagha—"bandits" by French definition, "patriots" according to the Neo-Destour—who wore regular army uniforms with the tabs of a "National Army of Liberation"; and life-for-life reprisals by French vigilantes calling themselves the Red Hand.

In the four months before Mendès-France's visit, the Fellagha had killed eighty-three civilians and soldiers, kidnapped twelve French officers, and lost two hundred of their own men. During the same period murder in the cities had become a mass affair. Seven Frenchmen were killed in Bizerte, for instance, when a Neo-Destourian group machine-gunned a European café, and the same number of Tunisians died in an Arab café near Sfax in a return raid organized by the Red Hand. . . .

Mendès-France proposed to meet this emergency by giving the Tunisians almost everything they were asking for. He offered them full control over their own affairs, but with two important conditions: that France must be permitted to "safeguard the peace in this part of the globe, which is ours" by retaining the direction of Tunisian national defense and foreign policy; and that the 180,000 French *colons* in the protectorate, having "earned the right to live and work in Tunisia," must be free not only to remain but also to "develop their economic activities in a climate of confidence and friendship."

The plan wasn't revolutionary. Robert Schuman had offered much the same terms in 1950 when he was Foreign Minister, and the Neo-Destour had accepted them. But Schuman's plan was shelved when the nationalist premier, after trying for the next two years to pin the French down on details, decided to take Tunisia's case to the United Nations, whereupon the resident general sent him and three members of his cabinet into exile in the desert. That was when the terrorism started. . . .

With substantial help from France, the French *colons* have done a great deal in Tunisia since the protectorate was established in 1881. Among other things, they have built 8,900 kilometers of roads, 2,500 kilometers of railroads, five major ports, and eight power stations. They have developed Tunisia's mines to produce 977,000 metric tons of iron a year, 34,000 metric tons of lead, and 2.3 million metric tons of phosphates. Much of this has been done to help the *colons,* of course, and the great majority of Moslems still live on the edge of starvation. Nevertheless, the French have put 154,000 Arab children into schools, provided five thousand hospital beds, and raised native consumption of bread by a third, tea and sugar by a half, cotton by two thirds, and meat by 280 per cent. . . .

It might have been possible, when Mendès-France became premier, for the French to hang on a good while longer, sending reinforcements for the fifty thousand troops already in Tunisia, providing arms for a civilian militia, and proceeding methodically with the *ratissages* —house-to-house military clean-ups—that have already aroused passionate hatred in native villages. As [Habib] Bourguiba [Tunisia's nationalist Neo-Destour leader] had warned, however, such a course seemed foredoomed to failure.

Mendès-France did more than accept these facts. He accepted them with such high style that he was able to carry off a politico-military operation of exquisite delicacy.

In making his offer to the Bey, he was already trying the *colons,* and many voters at home, to the limit of their endurance. He was crowding his luck by trying to negotiate an agreement with the Neo-Destour while Neo-Destourians were sniping daily at French citizens, and their brothers in the Fellagha Army were burning down French farms. If he insisted on dissolving the French Empire, as one Tunisian *colon* remarked in the Senate, he might at least demand the unconditional surrender of the Fellagha Army in advance.

Mendès-France could reasonably ask Neo-Destour leaders to call off their terrorists in the cities; he did, and they did. But it was asking a great deal—more than many Frenchmen realized—to demand that the Fellagha Army be disarmed and dispersed before any agreement was signed. . . .

Moreover, the Fellagha could not be disbanded easily, even by the Neo-Destour. The Tunisian Army of Liberation, said to number more than two thousand, was organized in small, mobile units spread over a vast mountainous terrain, with a few recognized chiefs but no central command. It included not only Neo-Destourians but also an assortment of independent nationalists—some as extremist as the Moslem Brotherhood in Egypt—and quite a few common outlaws who welcomed the protective covering of a "patriot's" uniform. Nationalists and outlaws alike had blood on their hands and a price on their heads; and most of them, having severed all ties with village and family, had neither job nor home to come back to. Above all, they were not sophisticated city people who could follow the subtleties of Franco-Tunisian relations. For the most part, their knowledge of this subject was limited to the muzzle of a French infantryman's rifle.

It was an extraordinary act of faith in a single man that the Neo-Destour should have undertaken to demobilize such an army under such circumstances, and Mendès-France realized it. . . .

The truce agreement was attacked violently from several sides. The *colons* said it was such proof of French weakness that it would simply encourage the Fellagha's resistance. The local Communist party called it treason and urged them to ignore it. So did the Arab League in Cairo. . . .

But the biggest chief of all, Lahsar Chraiti, came down. "This war between the French and us," he told journalists, "was like a father killing his son. A father would not kill his son, but defend him in his difficult hours. . . . I have confidence now in my government and the government of France. . . .

Algeria

The *colons* in Algeria claim they didn't have a problem until Mendès-France became premier. . . .

[On November 1, 1954] thirty attacks were carried out against the French population. In Algiers, the capital, terrorists left three bombs at the radio station and tried to set an oil depot on fire. Elsewhere they bombed public buildings, burned crops and haystacks, cut telephone wires, blew up bridges, and killed seven people.

The outbreak shocked France as nothing in Tunisia could have done. Algeria isn't simply a colony. It is the home of a million Frenchmen. It has been French territory since 1830, and an extension of metropolitan France since 1947, when a special statute was passed giving French citizenship to its 8 million Moslems and assigning thirty seats in the French Assembly to elected deputies representing Algeria's French and Moslem populations.

As far as most people knew in France, the statute had put an end to any nationalist agitation. The news on November 1, therefore, was not only shocking but astounding. The authorities at once rounded up several hundred suspected terrorists in the cities. But there remained a regular military formation of two or three thousand armed men calling themselves the Algerian Army of Liberation, entrenched in the wilderness of the most forbidding mountain range in North Africa, the Massif d'Aurès.

The first official explanation was that this army was made up mainly of Tunisian Fellagha who had come over the border less than a hundred miles away, that they were acting under orders from the Arab League, and that they were relying on broadcasts from Cairo and Budapest to stir up the local population.

There were several things wrong with this explanation. It turned out that no more than 150 Tunisians had come over the frontier; the rest were local men. There was no doubt that both the Voice of the Arabs beamed from Cairo, and the Budapest Arabic program—begun, significantly, six weeks earlier—represented an energetic effort to prod the Algerian Moslems into action. But very few villages in the indescribably poor and primitive Aurès had radios or even electricity.

If this was a genuine nationalist uprising, however, the timing was curious. Algeria was having one of the best crop years in history, which should have meant some prosperity for everyone. Just ten days earlier, the new Mendès-France government had sent its Interior Minister, François Mitterand, to the Algerian Assembly with a promise of a $100 million public-works and development program and progressive political reforms. Furthermore, this government was the first in years to show some understanding of Moslem aspirations, and was already negotiating with the Neo-Destour for Tunisia's autonomy. Why, after so many years of silence, open a terrorist campaign in Algeria at the moment best calculated to wreck the Moslems' hopes in Tunisia and destroy Mendès-France?

Even now, it isn't easy to answer these questions. But it seems plain that while there were several contradictory forces behind this operation, Mendès-France was its major target.

The Arab League is too xenophobic and extremist to approve of the Mendès-France policy in North Africa—a policy designed to keep 20 million Moslems loosely but loyally within the French orbit. For this reason, it fought the Neo-Destour aggressively during the weeks of Tunisian negotiations. In trying to provoke trouble in Algeria at this critical moment therefore, its motives were clear.

The same might be said for the Communists. They have very little influence in North Africa at present. But the longer the Moslems chafe under a harsh French administration, the more promising North Africa becomes for the policymakers of the Cominform.

The Algerian Moslems themselves weren't ready for the kind of rebellion the Arab League and Cominform might have liked to arrange. Nevertheless, they were more restless than the outward calm of Algeria had made them seem. The Arabs and Berbers here are forced, by a century of close association as well as by the Statute of Algeria, to accept the presence of the French. But it hasn't been easy for them. The statute had promised them universal free suffrage, cultural equality, municipal self-government, and an equal vote in the Algerian Assembly. None of these promises had been kept. Elections in Algeria are so cynically rigged that conservative MRP [Mouvement Républicain Populaire] deputies have denounced them in the Assembly as "intolerable"; and the Moslem deputies who are permitted to be elected are referred to contemptuously by the *colons* themselves as *"Beni-Oui-Ouis,"* or yes men, representing no one but themselves.

Over the last seven years, these practices have brought about the almost total eclipse of the moderate pro-French nationalist party, UDMA, led by Ferhat Abbas. Its place has been taken by the extremist MTLD, headed by an uncompromising agitator named Messali Hadj, who from his place of exile in France has been doing his best to prepare the Moslems for a war to the death against the French.

He has been directing an active political campaign for longer than the Governor General in Algiers cares to admit. In the "good" year of 1952, for instance, 920 MTLD members were arrested for sedition. But . . . [in September 1954] Messali announced that something worse was coming. It was time, he told *Le Monde,* for Algeria's case to be brought before the world, and this would require "direct action." . . .

There are persistent rumors in Algiers that some of the hardiest *colons* did what they could, in collusion with the lower echelons of the police, to help the revolt along, if only by failing to notice the clandestine movement of arms. Whether or not that is true, the November outbreak offered them the possibility of stopping Mendès-France both in Tunisia and Algeria, if not getting rid of him altogether. . . .

The Algerian *colons* are enormously influential in Paris, and can be deadly enemies. They are flatly opposed to any political reform. "The gravity of the situation," one of them said in the Assembly, "forbids any concessions that would permit troublemakers to claim a victory over France." They are convinced, and they may be right, that once Tunisia gets autonomy, there will be no stopping the nationalists in neighboring Algeria.

They are also convinced, and here they are almost surely wrong, that the only answer to these nationalists is preventive war.

[In February 1955 Mendès-France was voted out of office by the Assembly on the issue of his North African policies. See "End of a Ministry of Hope," in Section I, above.—Ed.]

THE NEW DIRECTION OF MOROCCO AND TUNISIA [6]

The men who led the peoples of Morocco and Tunisia in their successful struggle for independence, achieved only this past year, and who now direct the destinies of these new nations, are in a position like that of most successful candidates for political office: they have won

[6] From "North Africa Meets the Modern World," by Benjamin Rivlin, assistant professor of political science at Brooklyn College. *Commentary.* 22: 344-350. October 1956. Reprinted by permission.

and they have to produce. The platform upon which they ran was somewhat vague. Its ambiguities, even contradictions, created no particular problems and caused them no great concern in the midst of the fight for independence, when the sole objective was to win. But now that victory is theirs, these cannot be easily glossed over. What have the Moroccan and Tunisian nationalists promised their peoples, and what problems do these promises pose for the new governments? In particular, what sort of future can the non-Moslem minorities, notably the French and the Jews, look forward to in independent Morocco and Tunisia in the light of these promises and problems?

Moroccan and Tunisian nationalism were both based upon the conviction that French colonial rule was alien and oppressive. National independence would make it possible to replace this rule by self-government in accordance with native traditions and culture, and to substitute for an oppressive colonial administration a democratic regime with the welfare of the native population at heart. This was the double promise held out by the Moroccan and Tunisian nationalists. It was, obviously, a very general promise and admitted of a wide range of conflicting interpretation.

Alien rule is objectionable anywhere, but particularly so when imposed on a strongly traditional culture such as exists in Morocco and Tunisia. The Moslem-Arab tradition in North Africa stubbornly maintained itself despite all the Western influences introduced by the French. Fundamentally, it was the spirit of Islam that steeled this resistance, and the political expression of this spirit is what constitutes the essence of Tunisian and Moroccan nationalism. The latter's leaders therefore have no choice but to establish regimes consistent in temper with the Islamic and Arabic heritage of the two countries.

The second part of the nationalist program called for the creation of a democratic society. But what is meant specifically by "democratic"? The literature of North African nationalism overflows with professions of devotion to democracy, some of them vague and some of them not so vague. Typical of the latter is the following statement by Ahmed Balafrej, Secretary General of the Istiqlal party of Morocco and that country's new Foreign Minister, conveying as it does the aspirations of the more Western-oriented and liberal-minded leaders of the new regimes.

The Moroccan people [he writes in the April 1956 issue of *Foreign Affairs*] cherish the hope of exercising the attributes of effective sovereignty and of seeing a regime of liberty, equality and democracy established in their country. They expect to enjoy freedom of expression, thought, assembly and movement such as exists in independent sovereign nations. They aspire, in other words, to a respectable way of life. They think it will be assured by exploiting the country's riches efficiently and distributing them in a manner to raise the standard of living, absorb unemployment and guarantee quiet and well being for all. . . .

In Morocco and Tunisia, nationalism—as practically everywhere else—is in part a product of Western liberal thought. The ideal of democracy has, from the outset, been almost as much a source of inspiration for the nationalist movements in Tunisia and Morocco as the Islamic and Arabic ideal. Almost all the Tunisian Neo-Destour leaders and a good many of the Moroccan Istiqlal leaders are Paris-educated—which means that the French Revolution has been their school. . . .

The central importance of the democratic ideal to the new leaders of Tunisia and Morocco is reflected in a recent comment by Habib Bourguiba, Neo-Destour leader, upon taking office as Prime Minister of Tunisia:

The independence which we have bought at a price of great sacrifice will be an empty word if it does not come to signify at the same time the creation of a modern, democratic, and social state.

Still, pronouncements about democracy do not constitute democracy, no matter how often made; there is bound to be a gap between ideal and reality under the best of circumstances. How large will it be in Morocco and Tunisia? . . . It must not be forgotten that the North African nationalist parties are coalitions of groups of varying tendencies banded together in common opposition to foreign domination, not a doctrinaire, monolithic organization. Now that independence is a fact, each of these groups is bound to go off in its own direction, thus risking collision with other groups. . . .

For Moroccans and Tunisians, identification with Arab tradition means supporting other Arab peoples in their struggles for independence, and championing the unity of Arab interests everywhere. Many of today's leaders in Morocco and Tunisia were at one time under the influence of Shakeeb Arslan, the outstanding Pan-Arabist of the 1920's and 1930's, who encouraged Moroccan and Tunisian nationalism as incipient forms of Pan-Arab nationalism. Typical of this identification with the Arab world as a whole is a statement made by Sultan Mohammed V in Tangier on April 11, 1947:

Needless to say, Morocco is an Arab country closely attached to the Arab East; it is natural, therefore, that these ties should grow closer and stronger, particularly so since the Arab League has become an organization playing an important role in world politics.

As the North African nationalists' struggle for independence grew more intense during the past ten years, their ties with the Arab states became closer. Tunisian and Moroccan leaders have visited Egypt and other Arab countries frequently, conferring with Arab League leaders, and affirming their solidarity with the Arab world. A Maghreb [North African] office was opened in Cairo, and when the Moroccan and Tunisian questions came up before the United Nations the Arab member-states led the fight on behalf of the North Africans. . . .

It is just these "Arab feelings" that confront Morocco and Tunisia with two of their thorniest problems: Algeria and Israel. Responsible Moroccan and Tunisian leaders know that the task of establishing their nations on a firm foundation and coping with their social and economic problems is difficult enough without their becoming involved in situations outside the borders of their countries. Yet it is impossible for them, as Arab nationalists of some sort, not to get so involved.

Certainly this is true in regard to Algeria, with which Morocco and Tunisia have close historical and geographical bonds as well as a common hostility to France. Moroccans and Tunisians do not forget that their own struggles for independence were greatly helped by the embarrassment that the unrest in Algeria caused France. Indeed, the haste with which Morocco and Tunisia were granted their independence during the past year is in no small part attributable to the Algerian revolt: the French were eager to settle the situation in Morocco and Tunisia so as to have a free hand in Algeria. Now the Algerian rebels are asking for help in their turn—and getting it. The Moroccan and Tunisian governments have openly espoused the cause of the Algerian rebels and are presently trying with little success to prevent French troops from using their territory as a base of operations against the rebels.

As the fighting continues unabated in Algeria, the tension mounts in Morocco and Tunisia. . . . [On August 13, 1956] the Moroccan nationalist organ *El Alam* carried an appeal for funds to aid the Algerian rebels, declaring:

Islam ordains us to deliver our Moslem brothers from foreign bondage. Since Algeria finds itself in dire need of material and moral aid, some loyal citizens have decided to come to the aid of the *Moujahiddines* [fighters of a *jihad*—holy war] of a brother country. Moroccans must understand that the freedom of Algeria is the freedom of Morocco. . . .

Though Morocco and Tunisia are less directly involved in the matter of Israel and Zionism because of their geographical remoteness, they are nonetheless emotionally involved. For tactical reasons, neither country has joined the Arab League yet, but sooner or later they will. . . . [On April 22, 1956] Dr. Sadok Mokkadem, special envoy of the Tunisian government in the Middle East, declared in Damascus that

Tunisia, united with the other Arab countries by race, religion and language, will adhere to the Arab League and will participate in all activities undertaken by it on the international level in favor of Arabism and Islamism.

He said further that

Tunisia will align itself on the side of the Arab countries in the Palestine question because Zionism represents one of the aspects of imperialism.

In Morocco, though individual Jews are being permitted to emigrate, as well as those already in transit camps, organized emigration to Israel has been halted.

But even before the Algerian question exacerbated anti-French feeling, and the Israeli question anti-Jewish feeling, the position of these non-Moslem minorities was none too easy. The long years of French rule, and especially the vehemence with which the French "colonists" of Morocco and Tunisia opposed the nationalists, are not easily forgotten. As for the Jews, the inferior position assigned them in the traditional Islamic society that existed not so long ago in Tunisia and Morocco needs no repetition here.

Because the Algerian and Israeli issues directly affect the rights and security of minorities in Morocco and Tunisia, they illuminate what is perhaps the profoundest political and spiritual conflict facing these countries— the contest between the Arab-Islamic ideals and those of social and political democracy. This is not to imply that an Arab-Islamic society is inherently and necessarily undemocratic. But traditional Islamic society . . . inevitably runs into all sorts of difficulties in trying to transform itself into a modern liberal democracy.

It is a pity that Morocco and Tunisia have had to deal with the minorities question so early in their lives as independent states, without having the time to work it out in a calm and reasonable atmosphere. Nevertheless, both governments have indicated that they will not be stampeded into hasty action on this question. During the previously mentioned tour of Sultan Mohammed V, he and his son, Prince Moulay Hassan, met with representatives of the French and Jewish communities and went out of their way to promise them protection of their rights as Moroccans. Both in Tunisia and Morocco, despite the Islamic emphasis, the nationalist governments have made a point of having a Jewish minister in the government. . . .

The inclusion of Jews in the governments, the declaration of equal rights for all, and the invitation to the minorities to participate in the building of the new Moroccan and Tunisian nations are notable steps in the direction of democracy. But just as we have learned in the United States that a pronouncement by even the highest court in the land does not by itself abolish segregation, a long course of public reeducation being needed, so in Morocco and Tunisia the formal declaration of equal rights needs the real assent of the mass of the people themselves. And then the crucial question arises: if Islam is the official state religion, will there be any chance for such reeducation?

There is an additional obstacle in the way of the democratization of the position of minorities in Morocco and Tunisia: the policy of national integration pursued by leaders flushed with their new victory. Actually, the sense of national identity is a relatively new phenomenon in North Africa. To forge unified nations out of the separatist and particularist elements making up North African society requires the transcending of all the traditional subgroup affiliations (tribe, religious brotherhood, etc., etc.). But if—as is clearly the case in Morocco at least—integration is based on the spiritual tradition and ideal of Islam, how can the non-Moslem minorities make part of this unity? Even in Tunisia, where an important step in national integration has been taken on a basis not unfair to the non-Moslem minorities, the new constitution still proclaims Islam as the official state religion.

The history of nationalism throughout the world has shown that where there is militant nationalism, there is the danger too of what has been termed "integral" or "totalitarian" nationalism, a form of social organization quite incompatible with democracy. The true democratic ideal—of unity in diversity—is not easily achieved. Too extreme an approach by the Moslems of North Africa to the problem of national integration courts the danger of alienating the non-Moslem minorities, who will see it as a threat to their existence.

ALGERIA: THE STRANGLEHOLD OF
THE EXTREMISTS [7]

The reasons for the impasse in Algeria are painfully familiar. We have come across them before in Indo-China, in South Africa and in Kenya. In Indo-China, France failed to realize the dynamic upsurge of Asian nationalism and of anti-colonialism, just as in Algeria it has failed to respond to Moslem nationalism and resentment against all that is implied by colonial status. In Kenya, Mau Mau had its roots in land hunger, poverty and frustration, and in resentment against a minority of white settlers determined to maintain their privileged position. In South Africa, 3 million whites have committed themselves, in the name of Western civilization, to preserve their supremacy over 11 million non-whites. We find the same white settler attitude displayed by the French *colons* of Algeria.

Fewer than 1 million *colons* ["colonists" of French extraction] have sought, in the name of French culture, to preserve their higher status over 8 million non-French Moslem Algerians. It is true that French culture, technical and financial aid has done much to raise living standards in Algeria. It would be as wrong to overlook this unassailable fact as it would be to deny the failures of French policy.

The immediately outstanding fact is that after 120 years of French rule based on a policy of assimilation and of liberty, equality and fraternity there are not one but two Algerias: the one French, the other Moslem. French Algeria is relatively well-off and, in patches, very wealthy. Moslem Algeria is poor and, for the greater part, miserably so. About 1.5 million Algerians are

[7] From "Algeria—Can France Hold On?" by Colin Legum, African correspondent of the London *Observer*. *New Republic*. 134:9-11. April 9, 1956. Reprinted by permission.

entirely dependent on funds sent home by 300,000 Algerian workers in France.

The bulk of Algerians live on and off the land. But though they are outnumbered by eight to one, the *colons* own one third of all the arable land.

What of political rights? Formally, the position is that half the seats in the Algerian Assembly are reserved for French citizens (including assimilated Moslems) and the other half for the Moslems. In fact, the *colons* dominate the Assembly and maintain a powerful lobby in Paris: a lobby so powerful that it could truthfully boast of its role in overthrowing Mendès-France.

Successive French Governments have proved themselves unwilling or unable to break the stranglehold of the *colons,* whose shortsighted policies have encouraged the growth of frustrated non-French (though not necessarily anti-French) Moslem parties. Each time one of these parties has grown too strong (as in Kenya and South Africa) it has been suppressed at the behest of the *colons.*

The result is that each new party that has risen in place of a suppressed one has been progressively less moderate.

Extremism has become a vicious circle in Algeria. Each new phase of militancy by either the Moslems or the *colons* has been the signal for greater reaction by the other side. Increasing militancy caused by internal friction has been stimulated by external factors—such as the rise of Egypt as a fomentor of pan-Arab nationalism, and the defeat of France in Indo-China.

The *colons*—incensed by what they feel to be the "betrayals" in Indo-China, Tunisia and Morocco by a "weak and corrupt government in Paris"—have become no less rebellious than the Moslems.

The result is that France is now faced with two rebellions in Algeria: one by the Moslem nationalists, the other by the *colons*. Concession to either side inflames the other. Conciliation seems out of the question.

It is clear that unless France is prepared to adopt an equally tough attitude to both sides it will forfeit its position as a metropolitan power [i.e., a mother country]. So far, toughness has been largely reserved for the Moslems; attempts to be tough with the *colons* have always come to grief. . . .

There is, however, another question no less important. Has France's conversion come too late for reforms—no matter how radical—to halt the onslaught of the Moslem nationalists? The belated promise of reforms did nothing to save France in Indo-China. Is this to be the case also in Algeria? For an answer to this question we must examine the character and strength of the Algerian rebels.

The National Liberation Front is strongly entrenched and popularly supported. The peasants, either because they believe that the rebels will improve their lot or because they are terrorized, support the rebellion. For the time being, therefore, the rebels hold the tactical advantage in the struggle for the support of the rural masses. It is doubtful whether France can persuade the peasants to believe in its promised reforms so long as the rebels promise victory. This analysis, if it is accurate, suggests that before any reforms can be of value the power of the rebels must be broken. Already, France has committed almost a quarter of its total armed forces to achieve this.

The rebels are well-armed and growing in strength. Their present striking force is probably 12,000. Recruits are apparently plentiful; the limitation is that of arms. These are reaching Algeria through Libya from Egypt, and from Spanish Morocco. Much of the Algerian terrain is a gift from the gods to guerrilla fighters. And the rebels have good leaders. Their commander-in-chief is Mohammed ben Bella, a much-decorated *chef de section* of the French Army. His chief lieutenants include many well-trained junior officers.

Nor do the rebels fight alone. Their Cairo committee, headed by Mohammed Khider, a former Algerian deputy in the French parliament, is in close contact with the Egyptian government and with the Arab League. Radio Cairo gives powerful support to their cause. No wonder that Khider boasts: "It is not just the rebels who fought in Algeria; behind us are the Arab nations." And behind the Egyptian bloc, the Russians?

That is what the French believe. They claim that Russian arms are releasing Egyptian arms that are shooting down the French in Algeria. From this, the French argue that Russia is making a breach in the Western line of defense.

Arms are said to reach Algeria via Libya, the desert kingdom that is in the Western camp and offers facilities to the United States and Britain for important bases. France insists that Anglo-American action in Libya can cut the rebels off from Egypt and Russia. Such a claim overlooks Libyan sovereignty. There is good reason to suppose that if Libya were pushed too far it might "do a Jordan" on its allies.

From the analysis thus far it is clear that Algeria is not just a French problem. It represents an extension of the frontier in the present political conflict between the pan-Arab revolt (subtly egged on by Russia) and the Western powers. Anglo-American commitments to France cannot be isolated from that wider sphere. Mohammed Khider recently told a correspondent in Cairo: "Our people see French soldiers in American uniforms riding in American tanks—what do you expect them to think? They don't know anything about communism, so they are neutral about it."

[Khider, ben Bella, and three other rebel leaders were captured by the French in the fall of 1956, when a French-piloted airplane carrying them to a conference landed in Algeria.—Ed.]

The rebels are no longer willing to accept reforms to redress their wrongs—reforms which five years ago might have been welcomed with open arms. They now demand a fully independent Moslem state in Algeria: a demand inspired by the contemporary pan-Arab offensive and fired by religious fanaticism. It is difficult to see how France can deny to Algeria what it has conceded to Tunisia and Morocco. This is a vital question when one comes to consider if it is possible to detach the nationalists from this pan-Islamic Front. It is difficult to say. Certainly, a victory for the National Liberation Front would greatly strengthen the hand of Egypt and its allies, and would be hailed as a great Arab victory.

But what will be the consequences of a long and bitter struggle in Algeria, assuming—as one must—that the policy of reform will fail to deter the rebels? Such a struggle will keep the Arab cauldron boiling merrily, and will give incalculable opportunities for anti-Western propaganda which will further weaken United States, British and French influence in the Middle East and North Africa. It will strengthen Russia's propaganda in the Middle East and in Asia: "another colonial war." It will sap France and weaken its hold over its other African territories.

The disadvantages are indeed numerous. But we return to our original question: what are the alternatives? Clearly, France cannot abandon Algeria: its 900,000 *colons* don't permit of such a policy. Therefore, willy-nilly, it must fight. . . .

The political reforms must . . . await Algeria's pacification. Then the Algerians will be allowed free elections. But nothing is said about the form of these elections. Nor is there any clarity about whether the Moslem majority will be permitted to swamp the *colons'* minority. One thing is said, however. Algeria will never be free to declare its independence. While recognizing the right of Algerian nationhood, the Algerians will be free only to decide what form the "indissoluble links" with France will take. Once again, such a program would have been acclaimed by Algerian leaders five years ago. Today their attitude is much more doubtful. . . .

France must, for her own sake and for the sake of the Western alliance, lift Algeria out of the arena of "colonial warfare."

It has gone some way toward achieving this result. . . . But it must go further. And in doing so it is entitled to the fullest backing of the United States and Britain. But before such support can be honestly given, five steps must be taken:

1. The United States and Britain should make it clear that they will fully support France in helping to achieve a peaceful settlement in Algeria.

2. France must define precisely what political status Algeria is to be given. This should provide not only for Algerian nationhood to be accepted and respected, and for the minority rights of the *colons* to be safeguarded, but it should allow of Algeria's being linked as a free and equal partner of France.

3. France must show the same vigor in forcing the *colons* to accept the authority of the French parliament as it shows in its dealings with the nationalist rebels.

4. France must announce its willingness to negotiate with influential Moslem leaders (as opposed to the "stooges" in the Algerian Assembly) for a cease-fire and for the implementation of the promised reforms. Here the mediating services of Tunisian and Moroccan leaders would be useful.

5. The United States and Britain should be ready to associate themselves with France in underwriting these guarantees. And they should associate themselves with France in addressing a stern warning to Egypt to desist from giving any form of support to the rebels.

OUR STAKE IN NORTH AFRICA [8]

Americans have an unusually big stake in a peaceful atmosphere in seething North Africa. Officially, the United States government has taken a circumspect, hands-off policy toward French troubles in Morocco and Algeria but developments have been watched with great concern.

The United States has built four major air bases in French Morocco—at Sidi Slimane, Bennguerir, Boulhaut, and Nouasseur, each of which is militarily considered very important, or vital to the defense of the Western allies in the event of war.

Our Strategic Air Command operates forces from each of the four bases. The significance of these bases is underlined by the fact that as of today from these four points our war planes could reach, and destroy, certain key targets deep behind the Iron Curtain. These bases are so well placed that by utilizing them, our long-range bombers would not have to be refueled while winging over enemy territory.

[8] From "North Africa Perils Western Defense," by Sam Stavisky, writer on French and North African affairs for *Nation's Business*. *Nation's Business*. 43:54-8+. November 1955. Reprinted by permission.

In addition, Rabat, in French Morocco, is the site of the headquarters for the Seventeenth Air Force, commanding our Air Force units not only in North Africa, but in the Mediterranean and Middle East areas as well.

The Navy also maintains a major installation in French Morocco, at Port Lyautey, which also serves as an air base in support of our Seventh Fleet operations in the Mediterranean Sea. From the military point of view, French Morocco is one of the best—strategically located —areas available to the Air Force at this time. New bases are being built in Spain, but these are months away from completion and utilization.

Except for warfare with the Barbary Coast pirates between 1800 and 1815, the United States showed little interest in North Africa until World War II. Then, North Africa became the base for the assault on the European mainland via Sicily and Italy.

Since the development of the U.S. bases in Morocco, with French consent, the United States has maintained troops there, but the defense of the area and our installations is left to France.

The United States is naturally concerned lest civil war threaten the operation of the bases.

The United States is also concerned over the North African drain on French resources, especially military manpower. The French have already withdrawn three of the five divisions, which they had committed to NATO's line of defense on the European continent, to meet the situation in North Africa.

The French argue that, in defending North Africa, they are effectively defending the over-all interests of NATO. This argument has won little acceptance in the United States or NATO. . . .

The United States has a third important interest in North Africa. Our government has been long contending with Russia for the affections of the so-called neutral Arab and Asian states. Every action taken by the United States offending one of these states affects our relations with the others. Thus, while scrupulously avoiding open criticism of France, we have carefully avoided showing active hostility toward the North African nationalists.

Even so, the Moroccan nationalists are resentful toward the United States over two issues:

Rightly or wrongly, the nationalists believed that President Roosevelt orally promised the . . . sultan— during the Casablanca conference of 1943—that the United States would help Morocco regain its independence. Second the nationalists charge that the French have been fighting them in North Africa with American-contributed arms and equipment. . . .

Officially, the United States has to date taken what is tantamount to a hands-off policy.

In recent background memoranda on North Africa, the State Department expressed the official American position as follows:

Algeria:

The United States considers Algeria as an integral part of the French Republic. In the interest of Western security objectives, the United States welcomes all constructive steps taken by the French government to assure the internal stability of the area.

Tunisia:

We have the double objective not only of preserving our Mediterranean interests and our relations with France as a leading partner in NATO, but also of maintaining our traditional sympathy for self-government and our relations with the Arab and Asian states. We have therefore sought, in the United Nations and elsewhere, to promote an atmosphere in which France and Tunisia, free from outside interference, could work out solutions as to their outstanding differences

which would be voluntary, mutually acceptable, and therefore more durable.   The signing of the Franco-Tunisian
conventions justifies this attitude on our part. . . .

Morocco:

The principal objectives of the United States in Morocco
are to maintain the various national interests both direct and
indirect . . . and to contribute as far as possible to peace
and stability.   We sympathize with the aspirations of dependent peoples for a greater participation in their management of their own affairs, yet we recognize the importance
of French contributions to Morocco and the importance to
France, our partner in NATO, of her ties with Morocco.

Peace, stability, and political development in Morocco
are of great importance to the United States and to the
West because of our own interests and those of our allies
and partners, including both France and the friendly Arab
and Asian states.

Unofficially, the United States Government is gravely
concerned over the explosive threat hanging over North
Africa and has been earnestly urging the French Government to hasten reforms before it is too late, as happened
in the case of French rule in Syria, Lebanon, and in
Indo-China.

SUEZ: KEY TO THE FRENCH NORTH AFRICAN DILEMMA [9]

The violence of the French reaction to Egypt's
nationalization of the Suez Canal . . . strikingly demonstrated to the world the depth of feeling provoked here
[in Paris] by the inroads on France's position in North
Africa. . . .

Premier Nasser has become a major whipping boy
here.   He is regarded as an ambitious dictator who has
risked the peace of the world in order to satisfy his desire

<hr>

[9] From "French See Suez as Key to Their African Dilemma," by Henry
Giniger, special correspondent for the New York *Times*.   New York *Times*.
p E5.   September 9, 1956.   Reprinted by permission.

to expand his power throughout North Africa and the Middle East. He is the leading Arab spokesman for nationalism. His capital serves as headquarters for the Algerian rebellion. His radio has served as the vehicle of constant encouragement to the rebels and of constant vituperation against the French. His army is accused of training guerrilla leaders. Officials see evidence that some material aid to the rebels is coming or is being financed to some extent from Egypt.

No official will go so far as to say that if Egypt or President Nasser ceased to exist, the rebellion in Algeria would end tomorrow. It is contended, however, that Egypt's actions and attitudes enormously complicate the problems of restoring peace and of reaching an understanding with the Algerian Moslems. Robert Lacoste, the Resident Minister in Algeria, has therefore been led to warn the Government that unless President Nasser has been put in his place, the hope of an acceptable way out in Algeria will be dim. . . .

One gets the impression in reading the press and official statements that most Frenchmen feel that their country is fighting for its existence as a great power—a status that has been open to question since the German military crushed its armies in 1940. In the postwar period Frenchmen have been forced to witness without relish the break-up of French positions overseas. This process is now taking place at the point closest to home and one where French interests, economic and strategic, are more heavily concentrated than anywhere else.

France has put 400,000 men into Algeria to put down a rebellion that began on November 1, 1954, at a moment when the French Government was preparing to concede internal autonomy to neighboring Tunisia. Since then France has gone virtually all the way in concessions toward Tunisia. The same road was taken in Morocco, but in even more spectacular fashion, since there the Government was maneuvered into restoring a sultan it had chased from his throne two years previously.

Nationalism being an infectious thing, as most colonial powers have discovered, it has steadily gained ground in Algeria. In the beginning officials refused to recognize Algerian nationalism's legitimacy since it implied the existence of a nation. Algeria has been by fiat an integral part of the French nation, unlike Tunisia and Morocco, which conserved their status as states during the years France kept a tight grip on them.

But the spread of terrorism and disorder, the widening cleavage between Frenchmen and Moslems, the growing disaffection of even moderately disposed Moslems for France, has caused a significant change in official thinking. Implicit in this thinking is the feeling that there is sufficient legitimacy in the rebel action to justify a new political status for Algeria. . . .

Just as events in Tunisia and Morocco influenced events in Algeria, the reverse has become true. What started as an experiment in free cooperation between France on the one hand and Morocco and Tunisia on the other has now bogged down. The Tunisians and Moroccans have felt obliged to take up the Algerian nationalists' cause, thus putting a severe strain on their relations with France. The experiment has not failed, but it must remain inconclusive just so long as there are Moslems fighting France in Algeria.

EVENTS LEADING UP TO THE
MIDDLE EAST CRISIS [10]

Events in the Middle East had their genesis in the establishment of the State of Israel in 1948. The chronology that follows, starting with that event, lists the

[10] New York Times. p E5. November 4, 1956. Reprinted by permission.

developments that culminated in Israel's invasion of the
Sinai Peninsula and Anglo-French intervention for the
protection of the Suez Canal:

1948

May 14—British mandate in Palestine ends; independent state of Israel proclaimed. Arab armies immediately invade the new state.

1949

February 24—Armistice agreement between Israel
and Egypt ends war. Border incidents continue.

1950

July 9—Egypt prohibits ships bound for Israel from
using the Suez Canal.

1951

September 1—Egypt rejects United Nations resolution calling for an end to the blockade of Israeli ships.

1952

July 26—Coup led by General Naguib forces abdica-
tion of King Farouk.

1953

November 24—United Nations censures Israel for
attack on Jordan as border incidents continue.

1954

July 27—British agree to withdraw troops stationed
in Suez Canal area, as urged by Secretary of State Dulles.
Cyprus becomes main British base in Mideast.

November 1—Anti-French terrorism spreads to Algeria from Morocco and Tunisia, encouraged by Cairo.

November 14—Colonel Nasser becomes Egyptian head of government as General Nagiub is ousted.

1955

March 6—Syria joins in new military pact with Egypt and Saudi Arabia.

September 27—Colonel Nasser announces that Egypt will get arms from Soviet bloc.

1956

March 2—France recognizes independence of Morocco. King Hussein of Jordan dismisses John Bagot Glubb, British commander of the Arab Legion.

April 17—United Nations Secretary-General Hammarskjold goes to Mideast to settle continuing Arab-Israel border tension.

June 13—Last British troops leave Suez Canal zone.

June 23—Colonel Nasser, the only candidate, is elected President of Egypt.

July 19—United States withdraws offer to aid Egypt in building the Aswan High Dam.

July 26—President Nasser announces the nationalization of the Suez Canal Company.

August 21—Egypt rejects eighteen-nation plan, proposed by Dulles, that would place operation of the canal under an international board.

October 21—Jordan's elections end in victory for anti-West elements.

October 29—Israel attacks deep into the Sinai peninsula to wipe out bases for attacks by Egyptian terrorists.

October 31—Britain and France launch a joint attack on Egyptian bases for the announced purpose of guarding the Suez canal.

U.S. REACTION TO ANGLO-FRENCH INTERVENTION IN SUEZ [11]

At no time since the Korean war, and perhaps even since the Communist conquest of the Chinese mainland, have United States officials been confronted by a more serious situation than now faces them in the Middle East.

To put it bluntly, what faces them is that the Soviet Union has now emerged as the dominant power in that area, with the possibility, amounting to a probability, that it will be able to establish its authority in Syria and Egypt between West Europe and the vital oil supply of the Middle East.

This gloomy prospect, and how to dispel it, are now preoccupying official Washington more than the shorter-range question of how to establish a durable cease-fire under the United Nations along the Suez Canal.

Consequently, a debate of momentous proportions is now going on here behind the scenes. Some officials are taking the line that Britain and France, and not the United States, are responsible for the sudden deterioration in the West's position. They think Washington can do nothing more than keep pressing for a United Nations solution for the immediate situation.

Other officials, in contrast, are contending that only if President Eisenhower makes absolutely clear to Moscow that the United States will not tolerate the entrance of Soviet "volunteers" into the Middle East—indeed that

[11] From "Mideast Setback Alarms U.S. Aides," by James Reston, chief of the New York *Times* Washington bureau. New York *Times.* p 1+. November 14, 1956. Reprinted by permission.

Washington will counter any such move with similar moves of its own—can the situation be kept from declining into a disaster for the West. . . .

As of today, it is generally conceded here that the Soviet Union and Egypt have scored a tremendous victory. Britain and France have resorted to war and have failed to achieve their objectives of destroying the Egyptian dictator, President Gamal Abdel Nasser, or establishing their authority in the Suez Canal Zone.

Meanwhile, they have tarnished their moral position in the world. They have split with the United States, brought the United Nations down on themselves, and withdrawn in the face of what amounted to a Soviet ultimatum to halt their military activities or face the prospect of Soviet military intervention.

As most observers here see it, not only has there been a decline of the West's power in that area but the Soviet Union has emerged as the defender of the Arab world. The cry already is going out from Moscow to the Arabs to deny oil to the West and destroy all Western military bases in the entire region.

This, of course, affects not only Britain and France but also the United States, whose main bomber bases in Africa and the Middle East lie in Arab countries. It also affects Western Europe, whose factories and military forces get their oil from the Middle East. . . .

"If Colonel Nasser were to succeed, each one of us would be at the mercy of one man for the supplies on which we live," Prime Minister Eden told the House of Commons. "We could never accept that."

The situation now, however, after the British-French resort to arms, is as follows:

President Nasser has succeeded.

He got the British troops out of the Suez Canal base originally. He also maneuvered the British out of the Sudan. Furthermore, he succeeded in undermining British authority in Jordan. He has carried out a flood of anti-British and anti-French propaganda in Aden, Jordan, Bahrein, East Africa, Morocco, Tunis, and Algeria. He is now dictating the cease-fire terms, while the British and French troops stand around waiting for the end of the United Nations debate.

Meanwhile, the Soviet Union has won a great victory in an area it has been trying to penetrate for two centuries. Regardless of the outcome of the immediate controversy in the United Nations about the cease-fire, the Soviet leaders have staked out a new position in the Middle East that outflanks the West European oil supplies, and the Baghad Pact, which was a Middle Eastern extension of the North Atlantic alliance.

SUEZ: A BALANCE SHEET [12]

The British-French evacuation of Suez brings to an end a strange, dramatic episode that remains somewhat obscure as regards its origins but tragically clear as regards some of its immediate consequences.

Like a nuclear explosion, the destructive fall-out of which travels around the world, the British-French landing in Egypt was a local event with almost immeasurably far-reaching results.

It brought a shock to the Atlantic alliance. It brought a threat of Soviet military intervention in the Middle East.

[12] From article by Harold Callender, chief of the New York *Times* Paris bureau. New York *Times*. p5. December 22, 1956. Reprinted by permission.

It brought the Soviet Union and the United States into unwonted unison in the United Nations to demand a quick cease-fire.

It also threatened Western Europe with economic depression through an oil shortage. It precipitated a financial crisis in Britain.

Rarely if ever have such moderate forces landing in such a small area for so short a time set such potent political and economic forces in motion, upsetting a rough kind of balance that was not peace yet prevented open war.

It is difficult to isolate the effects of one nuclear explosion when it coincides with another. The British-French landing in Egypt early on November 5 came only a few hours after the Soviet Union's far more massive blow on November 4 at the Hungarian uprising, which threatened the balance of power in Europe, as the British-French landing threatened it in the Middle East.

Moscow's fury toward Britain and France may have owed something to its fears of satellite rebellion. Western anger at Britain and France owed much to the fact that they had divided and handicapped the West at the very moment the Soviet Union was running into trouble in Poland and Hungary.

Opposed by both the United States and the Soviet Union, which, from different motives, joined to reanimate the United Nations, Britain and France could only accept the demand for a cease-fire. They thus bowed to pressure such as no great power of the past felt it could accept without loss of status.

Britain lost her long preeminence in the Middle East, closely related to her Mediterranean position with her bases at Gibraltar, Malta and Cyprus.

The decline of her former imperial power, hitherto gradual, undramatic, almost painless, now entered a sudden, violent and more embarrassing stage as her dependence upon United States diplomatic and financial support was advertised for all to see. . . .

The Suez crisis divided the British people and shook their political life to its foundations. But it compelled Britain to take stock of her economic perils and to take a new resolve to eliminate them.

Britain was the hardest hit by the oil shortage, reducing Western Europe's supplies by 25 per cent or more. France was likewise hit, but the more visible setback for France so far has been political. The theory of her Government was that by a blow at President Gamal Abdel Nasser of Egypt, France could facilitate a solution of her North African problems, especially in Algeria where the rebels had been armed by Egypt.

But President Nasser remains in power and even bullies the United Nations, as the French see it.

So the Suez expedition failed of its major objective, and France must face the North African problem in Algiers, Tunis and Rabat, not in Cairo. Steps have been taken to grant Moslems equality in Algerian municipalities and eventually elsewhere. The result may be a North African federation of Algeria, Tunisia and Morocco. Thus the setback in Suez may have obliged France to act more realistically in North Africa while obliging Britain to do so in her economic policy.

France will lose at the rate of $300 million a year in oil taxes as a result of the shortage. Her trade with Egypt, Syria, Iraq and their neighbors will suffer.

She already had a foreign trade deficit running to about $800 million for this year but had in October about $1.4 million in gold and dollar reserves. Her financial crisis will not equal Britain's but her price level may be imperiled.

If Britain and France have been compelled by their Suez venture to face problems hitherto veiled or evaded, so has the United States. Acting through and outside the United Nations, Washington vetoed the British-French method of dealing with the Suez Canal and the Israeli-Egyptian quarrel.

Logic, at least European logic, therefore obliges Washington to find an alternative method. It seems to be up to the United States more than to any other Western nation to see that the canal, blocked by sunken ships, is not blocked also by President Nasser's tactics or by the slow adaptation of the United Nations to an unfamiliar task.

It seems to be mainly up to the United States to lead the West in seeking a permanent regime for the canal assuring its availability to all, and in seeking some international settlement to check the Middle Eastern ferment.

British and French leaders contend that their abortive expedition to Suez destroyed Soviet war material in Egypt and thus nipped a Soviet scheme to dominate the Middle East. Others contend that the expedition upset a crude sort of balance of power there that neither the United States nor the Soviet Union wanted to upset.

The Soviet Union may have gained in the Middle East from the division of Western policy that the expedition revealed. Yet the Soviet Union suffered everywhere from the division within its empire shown at Budapest.

This division may keep Moscow busy for a while and defer further Soviet pushes in the Middle East. Or it may lead to a new tension between East and West in Europe that would affect the Middle East. This would perhaps seem to indicate all the more reason for defining Western policies in both regions.

BIBLIOGRAPHY

BOOKS AND PAMPHLETS

An asterisk (*) preceding a reference indicates that the article or a part of it has been reprinted in this book.

Aron, Raymond. France and Europe. (Human Affairs Pamphlet no41) 24p. Henry Regnery Co. Chicago. '49.

Brinton, Crane. Temper of Western Europe. 118p. Harvard University Press. Cambridge, Mass. '53.

Brogan, D. W. France under the republic; the development of modern France (1870-1939). 844p. Harper & Bros. New York. '40.

Brogan, D. W. French personalities and problems. 240p. Alfred A. Knopf. New York. '47.

Brogan, D. W. Idea of European union. (Montague Burton Lecture on International Relations no8) 15p. Leeds. London. '49.

Earle, E. M. ed. Modern France; problems of the Third and Fourth Republics. 522p. Princeton University Press. Princeton, N.J. '51.

French Embassy Press and Information Division. Address by Christian Pineau before the U.N. General Assembly on November 22, 1956. 11p. The Division. 972 Fifth Ave. New York 21. '56.

French Embassy Press and Information Division. France moves forward: the story of economic and technical progress. 71p. The Division. 972 Fifth Ave. New York 21. '54.

French Embassy Press and Information Division. French policy in North Africa. Paul Reynaud. 3p. The Division. 972 Fifth Ave. New York 21. '55.

French Embassy Press and Information Division. French Union: political and administrative structure. 30p. The Division. 972 Fifth Ave. New York 21. '55.

French Embassy Press and Information Division. Text of interview granted by M. Guy Mollet to London Daily Herald on September 26, 1956. The Division. 972 Fifth Ave. New York 21, N.Y. '56.

Furniss, E. S. Jr. France: keystone of Western defense. (Doubleday Short Studies in Political Science 3) 77p. Doubleday & Co. New York. '54.

Furniss, E. S. Jr. Weaknesses in French foreign policy-making. 52p. Princeton University Center of International Studies. Princeton, N.J. '54.

Gavin, Catherine. Liberated France. 292p. St Martin's Press. New York. '55.

Godfrey, E. D. Jr. Fate of the French non-Communist Left. (Doubleday Short Studies in Political Science 15) 79p. Doubleday & Co. New York. '55.

Goguel, François. France under the French Republic. 198p. Cornell University Press. Ithaca, N.Y. '52.

Huddleston, Sisley. France: the tragic years, 1939-1947. 360p. Devin-Adair. New York. '55.

Landau, Rom. France and the Arabs. (Behind the Headlines. v 13, no 7) 16p. Canadian Institute of International Affairs. 230 Bloor St. W. Toronto 5. '54.

Liebling, A. J. Republic of silence. 522p. Harcourt, Brace & Co. New York. '47.

Luethy, Herbert. France against herself; tr. by Eric Mosbacher. 476p. Frederick A. Praeger. New York. '55.

McClellan, G. S. Middle East in the cold war. (Reference Shelf. v23, no6) 201p. H. W. Wilson Co. New York. '56.

McKay, D. C. United States and France. 334p. Harvard University Press. Cambridge, Mass. '51.

Malraux, André. Case for de Gaulle; a dialogue between André Malraux and James Burnham. 87p. Random House. New York. '48.

Matthews, Ronald. Death of the Fourth Republic. 318p. Frederick A. Praeger. New York. '54.

Munro, Katharine. France yesterday and today; a short survey. 107p. Royal Institute of International Affairs. London. '45.

Padover, S. K. France: setting or rising star? 64p. (Headline Series no81) Foreign Policy Association. New York. '50.

Padover, S. K. French institutions; values and politics. (Stanford University. Hoover Institute and Library on War, Revolution and Peace. Studies, Series E: Institutions) 102p. Stanford University Press. Stanford, Calif. '54.

Pickles, Dorothy. French politics: the first years of the Fourth Republic. 302p. Royal Institute of International Affairs. London. '53.

Rémy (pseudonym of Gilbert Renault Roulier) Memoirs of a secret agent of Free France; tr. by L. C. Sheppard. 406p. McGraw-Hill Book Co. New York. '48.

Roe, F. C. Modern France: an introduction to French civilization. 288p. Longmans, Green & Co. New York. '56.

Schuman, Robert. French policy towards Germany since the war. 24p. Oxford University Press. New York. '54.

Thomson, David. Democracy in France; the Third Republic. 283p. Oxford University Press. New York. '46.

Werth, Alexander. Twilight of France, 1933-1940; ed. by D. W. Brogan. Harper & Bros. New York. '42.

Williams, P. M. Politics in post-war France. 500p. Longmans, Green & Co. New York. '54.

Wright, Gordon. Reshaping of French democracy. 277p. Reynal and Hitchcock. New York. '48.

PERIODICALS

America. 91:157-9. My. 8, '54. Fourth Republic; ideology vs. politics. F. P. Canavan.

America. 91:395-6. Jl. 17, '54. Ominous shift in balance of power.

America. 92:447-50. Ja. 29, '55. Colonial peoples come of age.

America. 92:522, 530-2. F. 19, '55. Temper and tangles of French politics; with editorial comment. R. G. Neumann.

America. 94:91. O. 22, '55. French politics and North Africa.

America. 94:121. O. 29, '55. Colonialism and the Christian conscience.

America. 95:12. Ap. 7, '56. American support of France.

America. 95:258-9. Je. 9, '56. Algerian crisis.

American Political Science Review. 50:321-38. Je. '56. Communist presence in France. E. D. Godfrey.

Annals of the American Academy of Political and Social Science. 288:63-6. Jl. '53. Meaning of NATO for France and Europe. Jean de Lagarde.

Annals of the American Academy of Political and Social Science. 295:37-9. S. '54. America in European eyes. Jacques Freymond.

Annals of the American Academy of Political and Social Science. 298:109-16. Mr. '55. Context and sources of political tensions in French North Africa. Benjamin Rivlin.

*Annals of the American Academy of Political and Social Science. 306:10-16. Jl. '56. Aspirations of the people of French North Africa. Muhammad El-Farra.

Annals of the American Academy of Political and Social Science. 306:17-25. Jl. '56. Role of France and the French in North Africa. Roger Vaurs.

Antioch Review. 14:131-48. Je. '54. France: collapse of a class. E. D. Godfrey.

Atlantic Monthly. 192:51-4. Jl. '53. French in North Africa. Augustin Guillaume; tr. by G. L. Howe.
    Discussion. 192:31-2. O. '53.

Atlantic Monthly. 194:15-18. S. '54. Report on the world today.

*Atlantic Monthly. 197:60-5. My. '56. Crisis of French colonialism. Herbert Luethy.

British Survey. Main Service. p 13-24. Mr. '55. Enigma of France: political instability in an orderly country. Barley Adison.

Business Week. p54-5. Ja. 2, '54. New chance for France.

Business Week. p28-9. O. 15, '55. History is plunging ahead too fast for France.

Cambridge Journal. 7:36-50. O. '53. Crisis in France: a political institution. Philip Williams.

Catholic World. 177:378-82. Ag. '53. From my window in Fleet Street. Michael de la Bedoyere.

Christian Century. 70:1014-16. S. 9, '53. France and the U.S.A.?

Christian Century. 70:1285. N. 11, '53. France goes round and round.

Christian Century. 72:104-5. Ja. 26, '55. Western Europe and Catholic politics.

Christian Century. 72:1196. O. 19, '55. What lies ahead for France?

Christian Century. 73:919-20. Ag. 8, '56. Franco-Algerian war. G. W. Shepherd.

*Collier's. 133:19-23. Ja. 22, '54. France needs a new revolution. E. A. Mowrer.

Commentary. 16:1-9. Jl. '53. Is the free West in decline? Hans Kohn.

Commentary. 17:431-8. My '54. France's new parochial nationalism. Herbert Luethy.

Commentary. 18:118-26, 233-9. Ag.-S. '54. Morocco's Jews enter the 20th century. H. A. Lehrman.

Commentary. 18:285-95. O. '54. What Mendès-France's "new deal" stands for: gravedigger of the European idea? Herbert Luethy.

Commentary. 19:356-63. Ap. '55. Fall of Mendès-France's ministry of hope. Herbert Luethy.

Commentary. 20:393-402. N. '55. Morocco's Jews between Islam and France. H. A. Lehrman.

Commentary. 21:301-10. Ap. '56. Poujade: Hitler or Pierrot; tr. by M. J. Goldbloom. Herbert Luethy.

*Commentary. 22:344-50. O. '56. North Africa meets the modern world. Benjamin Rivlin.

Commonweal. 60:307-8. Jl. 2, '54. Europe's disaffection.

Commonweal. 61:87-9. O. 29, '54. Mendès-France; with editorial comment. Robert Barrat.

Commonweal. 61:419. Ja. 21, '55. Mendès-France performance.

Commonweal. 61:627-8. Mr. 18, '55. Why Mendès-France was defeated. Robert Barrat.

Commonweal. 63:635-8. Mr. 3, '56. American experiment through French eyes. Thomas Molnar.

Commonweal. 64:70-1. Ap. 20, '56. Crisis in Algeria. Robert Barrat.

Commonweal. 64:606-8. S. 21, '56. Burden of Algeria. Robert Barrat.

Confluence. 4:421-31. Ja. '56. Aid given by the mother country to colonized peoples: the example of France. Maurice Duverger.

Current History. 23:38-42. Jl. '52. European army treaty; summary with text of three-power statement.

Current History. 26:228-34. Ap. '54. France in Africa. A. Z. Rubinstein.

Current History. 28:257-63. My. '55. French politics and world affairs. E. D. Ellis.

Current History. 28:264-9. My. '55. French economic foundations. Alzada Comstock.

Current History. 28:288-98. My. '55. French empire II: Africa. A. Z. Rubinstein.

Current History. 28:299-304. My. '55. France and NATO. R. N. Berkes.

Current History. 28:304-9. My. '55. Selection from the Yalta conversations, dealing with France's role in post-war European affairs.

Current History. 30:368. Je. '56. Focus on French North Africa.

Economist. 169:183-4. O. 17, '53. France and American aid.

Economist. 169:592-3. N. 21, '53. From first to second Monnet plan.

Economist. 174:545-6. F. 12, '55. France without Mendès.

Economist. 177:1162. D. 31, '55. Algeria and the French voter.

Economist. 178:641. Mr. 24, '56. Algerian shadow over Paris.

Editorial Research Reports. v2, no23:865-81. D. 16, '53. French political instability. W. T. Stone.

Editorial Research Reports. v2, no 11:635-52. S. 15, '55. Future of France in North Africa. W. T. Stone.

Encounter. p23-31. My. '54. Democracy and its discontents: France. Herbert Luethy.

Fabian International Review. p8-11. My. '55. France after Mendès-France. Dorothy Pickles.

Foreign Affairs. 30:145-51. O. '51. France, still the Third Republic. Raymond Aron.

*Foreign Affairs. 31:349-60. Ap. '53. France and Europe. Robert Schuman.

Foreign Affairs. 32:365-73. Ap. '54. France and the defense of Europe: a French Socialist view. Guy Mollet.

Foreign Affairs. 32:374-82. Ap. '54. Rise and fall of the Anglo-French entente. André Géraud.

Foreign Affairs. 33:17-27. O. '54. Postscript to E.D.C. H. F. Armstrong.

Foreign Affairs. 33:111-22. O. '54. Political instability in France. François Goguel.

Foreign Affairs. 33:225-38. Ja. '55. France's new hope. Jean Hoffmann.

*Foreign Affairs. 34:394-404. Ap. '56. Stable instability in France. André Siegfried.

*Foreign Policy Bulletin. 32:58. Je. 1, '53. Constitutional reform in France. Gordon Wright.

Foreign Policy Bulletin. 33:7-8. Jl. 15, '54. End of illusions in France. V. M. Dean.

Foreign Policy Bulletin. 33:13+. Ag. 15, '54. Franco-American crisis. Neal Sanford.

Foreign Policy Bulletin. 34:12+. O. 1, '54. After EDC, what? V. M. Dean.

*Foreign Policy Bulletin. 34:20-2. O. 15, '54. French policy: right or wrong? H. L. Matthews; S. K. Padover.

Foreign Policy Bulletin. 34:25-6. N. 1, '54. What Europe thinks of unity: France. Roy Pierce.

Foreign Policy Bulletin. 34:92. Mr. 1, '55. Dropping the pilots: Paris and Moscow. V. M. Dean.

*Foreign Policy Bulletin. 35:49-50. D. 15, '55. France in crisis. S. K. Padover.

Fortnightly. 175(new series169):379-84. Je. '51. Origins of modern France. David Thomson.

Fortune. 51:114-15+. Je. '55. France's precarious prosperity. Michael Heilperin.

Harper's Magazine. 210:25-32. Ja. '55. Future of Mendès-France. Edmond Taylor.

*Harper's Magazine. 212:71-6. My. '56. Why the French act that way. H. L. Turtledove.

International Affairs. 30:148-55. Ap. '54. France's political and economic problems. Antoine Pinay.

International Conciliation. 495:195-256. N. '53. French union: concept, reality and prospects. Georges Catroux.

International Journal. 9:96-106. Spring '54. France and the European defense community. John Goormaghtigh.

International Journal. 9:282-94. Autumn '54. France, Tunisia and Morocco. Georges Catroux.

Journal of Politics. 15:399-423. Ag. '53. Internationalism, party politics, and the new French constitution. D. R. Deener.

Life. 37:84-90+. Jl. 19, '54. For immobilized France a man of change. E. J. Hughes.

Life. 39:98-100+. D. 19, '55. Why France is seldom free of crisis. Herbert Luethy.

Look. 19:50-2. N. 15, '55. Africa: the North explodes. E. M. Korny.

Look. 20:77-9+. Mr. 20, '56. What's the matter with France? E. M. Korny.

Middle East Affairs. 6:229-48. Ag. '55. Morocco, Tunisia and Algeria before the United Nations. H. C. Atyeo.

Nation. 177:33. Jl. 11, '53. France and Germany. Julio Alvarez del Vayo.

Nation. 179:146-7. Ag. 21, '54. Mendès-France, Europe's last reserve. Alexander Werth.

Nation. 179:253-4. S. 25, '54. Defeat of EDC: French view. Alexander Werth.

Nation. 180:233-4. Mr. 19, '55. France's new Left: what it is and what it needs. Julio Alvarez del Vayo.

Nation. 180:325-6. Ap. 16, '55. S.O.S. to the youth of France. François Mauriac.

Nation. 181:314. O. 15, '55. Fiasco in France. Alexander Werth.

Nation. 181:478-80. D. 3, '55. France's unique Left. Raymond Barrillon.

Nation. 182:213. Mr. 17, '56. Algerian dilemma. Alexander Werth.

Nation. 183:189-90. S. 8, '56. Dreams of imperial grandeur.

Nation. 183:194-5. S. 8, '56. Talk with Bourguiba. Alexander Werth.

Nation's Business. 42:70-6. O. '54. Our front against Reds hinges on French comeback. Herbert Harris.

*Nation's Business. 43:54-8+. N. '55. North Africa perils Western defense. Sam Stavisky.

New Leader. p3-6. N. 7; p20-1. N. 14, '55. Crisis in North Africa.

New Leader. p6-7. N. 7, '55. Maghreb (Northwest Africa) seeks unity. Keith Irvine.

New Republic. 130:11-13. Ap. 19, '54. French will fight for the West if . . . . Frank Gorrell.

New Republic. 131:6. Ag. 16, '54. Capacity to choose. Frank Gorrell.

New Republic. 131:9-12. S. 20, '54. North Africa: France's last chance. Ray Alan.

New Republic. 132:8. Ja. 3, '55. Corps de ballet. Frank Gorrell.

New Republic. 132:4. F. 7, '55. Opening windows in France. Frank Gorrell.

New Republic. 132:4. F. 21, '55. France: the unpalatable taste of truth. Frank Gorrell.

New Republic. 132:4. Mr. 7, '55. Back to the Third Republic. Frank Gorrell.

New Republic. 132:4. Mr. 21, '55. German rearmament: playing for delay. Frank Gorrell.

*New Republic. 134:9-11. Ap. 9, '56. Algeria: can France hold on? Colin Legum.

New Statesman and Nation. 50:848. D. 24, '55. France's secret war. K. S. Karol.

New Statesman and Nation. 51:754. Je. 30, '56. Last stand of the Stalinists. Pierre Hervé.

*New York Times. p 10. Ag. 31, '54. Project for EDC begun in France. Lansing Warren.

*New York Times. p20. Ag. 31, '54. Defeat for EDC; editorial.

*New York Times. p5. O. 4, '54. Text of final act of nine-power conference held in London between September 28 and October 3 (1954).

New York Times. p 1. D. 31, '54. French Assembly, 287-260, approves Western European Union accord, reversing earlier rejection.

*New York Times. p3. Ja. 9, '56. Red vote in France. Harold Callender.

*New York Times. p3. Ja. 10, '56. Paradox in France. Harold Callender.

*New York Times. p 14. Ag. 4, '56. Age of giants is over—III: France. C. L. Sulzberger.

*New York Times. p E3. S. 9, '56. French see Suez as key to their African dilemma. Henry Giniger.

*New York Times. p E5. N. 4, '56. Events leading up to the Middle East crisis.

*New York Times. p 1+. N. 14, '56. Mid-East crisis alarms U.S. aides. James Reston.

*New York Times. p5. D. 22, '56. Suez: a balance sheet. Harold Callender.

*New York Times. p F 1. Ja. 20, '57. Strength in unity sought by Europe. Harold Callender.

*New York Times. p 1+. Ja. 23, '57. Mollet wins vote in move for common market pact. R. C. Doty.

New York Times Magazine. p 10+. My. 31, '53. Behind the stalemate of French politics. T. H. White.

New York Times Magazine. p9+. Ag. 23, '53. Great revolution lives on in France. D. W. Brogan.

New York Times Magazine. p 13+. N. 1, '53. France inhibited by old habits. Harold Callender.

*New York Times Magazine. p9+. My. 16, '54. Can the Western three ride the storm? D. W. Brogan.

New York Times Magazine. p 10-11+. Ag. 15, '54. French empire: time runs out. D. W. Brogan.

New York Times Magazine. p9+. S. 26, '54. Still Europe's riddle: France and Germany. D. W. Brogan.

*New York Times Magazine. p 12+. Mr. 6, '55. In defense of the French. Janet Flanner (Genêt).

New York Times Magazine. p 15+. O. 16, '55. If France is to meet the challenge. Harold Callender.

New York Times Magazine. p 14+. O. 23, '55. Algeria: from a correspondent's notebook. Hal Lehrman.

New York Times Magazine. p8+. Ja. 1, '56. France converts in France's way. Harold Callender.

New York Times Magazine. p 12-13. Ja. 29, '56. L'assemblée nationale in session.

New York Times Magazine. p 12-13. F. 19, '56. Struggle in Algeria.

New York Times Magazine. p8-9. Je. 17, '56. Algerian maelstrom.

New Yorker. 32:124-5. F. 25; 70+. Je. 2; 123-4+. Je. 9; 78-80. Ag. 25; 79-80+. S. 15, '56. Letter from Paris. Genêt (Janet Flanner).

Newsweek. 41:42-3. F. 16, '53. Monnet, Europe's no. 1 man of ideas and hope.

Newsweek. 42:34. Jl. 6, '53. Cure for France; interview. Paul Reynaud.

Newsweek. 42:38-9. Ag. 24, '53. New unity in Europe. E. K. Lindley.

Newsweek. 44:41-3. Ag. 16, '54. Too little too late? North Africa. Benjamin Bradlee.

Newsweek. 45:24. Ja. 3, '55. France: is there real power to rule?

Newsweek. 45:36. My. 30, '55. Time's running out in North Africa.

Newsweek. 46:48. S. 26, '55. Unending crisis.

Newsweek. 47:29-32+. Ja. 16, '56. Dilemma of France; illusion of empire shattered, what comes now?

Newsweek. 47:34. F. 6, '56. Through the maze.

Newsweek. 47:38+. F. 20, '56. Algeria: more war before peace?

Newsweek. 47:36+. Mr. 5, '56. Even from the devil.

Newsweek. 47:42. Ap. 16, '56. France and Algeria: the tragic fact.

Newsweek. 47:34+. Je. 4, '56. Grim end to a time of hope.

Political Quarterly. 25:258-72. Jl. '54. Constitutional reform in France. Boris Mirkine-Guetzevitch.

Political Quarterly. 26:236-45. Jl. '55. Dilemma in French thought. Dorothy Pickles.

Political Science Quarterly. 65:335-52. S. '50. De Gaulle and the R.P.F. G. C. Cook.

Political Science Quarterly. 69:161-83. Je. '54. France in Europe: prospect and retrospect. René Albrecht-Carrié.

*Reader's Digest. 64:117-22. My. '54. What's wrong with France? Guy de Carmoy.

Reporter. 8:12-16. Mr. 3, '53. Pinay to Mayer to whom? T. H. White.

Reporter. 9:18-21. D. 22, '53. France: politicians, pressure groups and a new face. T. H. White.

Reporter. 10:19-22. Mr. 30, '54. Communists' new look in France. Edmond Taylor.

Reporter. 11:2. S. 14, '54. PMF and FDR.

*Reporter. 11:16-20. D. 30, '54. North Africa: bloody fingers and the loosening grip. Claire Sterling.

Reporter. 12:33-34+. F. 10, '55. Mendès-France and the republican tradition. André Fontaine.

Reporter. 12:4-5. Mr. 10, '55. Return to yesterday.

Reporter. 13:8-13. D. 29, '55. That man Mendès-France and France's destiny. Edmond Taylor.

Reporter. 14:2+. My. 17, '56. Plight of France.

Reporter. 15:31-6. Jl. 12, '56. Africa: we had better mean what we say. Chester Bowles.
    Discussion. 15:6-7. S. 20, '56.

Reporter. 15:17-20. O. 18, '56. Our diplomatic defeats and the unity of Europe. Edmond Taylor.

Reporter. 15:27-31. N. 1, '56. Can the French save their republic? André Fontaine.

Review of Politics. 16:412-37. O. '54. Crisis in French foreign policy. J. B. Duroselle.

Review of Politics. 17:295-328. Jl. '55. Neutralism in France. J. T. Marcus.

Round Table. 42:37-42. D. '51. A European army: the Pleven plan and its implications.

Saturday Evening Post. 225:40-1+. Ap. 11, '53. We're all fouled up in France. J. P. O'Donnell.

Saturday Evening Post. 227:12. Ag. 21, '54. We can't expect Europe to shed all her ancient hatreds at once.

Saturday Evening Post. 227:17-19+. My. 28, '55. Crisis in North Africa. E. O. Hauser.

Senior Scholastic. 63:7-9. Ja. 20, '54. France, key to Europe's deadlock.

Senior Scholastic. 65:12-15. S. 22, '54. France rolls from crisis to crisis. I. D. Talmadge.

Senior Scholastic. 67:9-11. N. 10, '55. France walks a tightrope.

Senior Scholastic. 67:14. Ja. 19, '56. Wanted: French unity.

Senior Scholastic. 68:12. F. 23, '56. France split on Algeria.

Senior Scholastic. 68:17. Mr. 15, '56. Three French problems.

Senior Scholastic. 68:12. Mr. 22, '56. North Africa, tinderbox.

Spectator. 193:515-16. O. 24, '54. Mendès-France—past and future. D. R. Gillie.

Spectator. 195:885-6. D. 30, '55. French elections. D. W. Brogan.

Time. 64:21-2. Ag. 16, '54. Old order changes; new rebellion; second look.

Time. 64:60+. N. 8, '54. Report on France.

*Time. 65:24-5. F. 14, '55. 233 days of Mendès-France.

Time. 65:16-17. F. 28, '55. French assembly; the curse of factions.

Time. 65:38. Mr. 28, '55. Reform or perish.

Time. 65:22-3. Ap. 11, '55. Fraternité, réalité.

Time. 65:25. My. 30, '55. Narrow choice in North Africa.

Time. 65:35-6. Je. 27, '55. Dangerous middle.

*Time. 66:20-1. Jl. 4, '55. French presence in North Africa. Raymond Aron.

Time. 66:18-19+. S. 5, '55. Conflict of sympathies; revolt and revenge.

Time. 66:31. S. 12, '55. U.S. is France's most faithful friend.

Time. 66:36-7. S. 12, '55. Violence and vacillation.

Time. 67:18-19. Ja. 2, '56. Tomorrow's secret.

Time. 67:22. Ja. 23, '56. Socialist to reckon with.

Time. 67:20. F. 13, '56. Algeria hurdle.

Time. 67:35. My. 21, '56. Fifth republic.

Time. 68:21. Ag. 6, '56. Reform that failed.

Time. 68:16-17. Ag. 13, '56. Angry challenge and response.

Time. 68:40. S. 10, '56. Chance for Algeria.

Town Meeting (Bulletin of America's Town Meeting of the Air). 20, no 13:1-15. Jl. 27, '54. How can we resolve U.S.-French differences? M. J. Ronant and Georges-Henri Martin.

Town Meeting (Bulletin of America's Town Meeting of the Air). 21, no29:1-12. N. 13, '55. What is the future role of France in Europe? Robert Valeur and Quincy Howe.

U.S. News & World Report. 34:46+. Mr. 13, '53. War III; would France fight? Interview. Raymond Aron.

U.S. News & World Report. 35:26. Ag. 21, '53. Decline of French power shakes Western alliance.

U.S. News & World Report. 35:64-72. N. 20, '53. Coming, a United States of Europe; interview. Paul Reynaud.

U.S. News & World Report. 36:28-9. My. 21, '54. U.S. allies getting weaker.

U.S. News & World Report. 36:120. Je. 4, '54. France we don't know. David Lawrence.

U.S. News & World Report. 37:132. O. 1, '54. Common danger. David Lawrence.

U.S. News & World Report. 39:80-2. Jl. 1, '55. France will stand by her allies; excerpts from address. Antoine Pinay.

U.S. News & World Report. 40:53-6. Ja. 13, '56. In France, pattern for revolution.

U.S. News & World Report. 40:40+. F. 10, '56. Where U.S. stands now with France.

U.S. News & World Report. 40:36. Mr. 16, '56. Coexistence speech that rocked the West; address, March 2, 1956 by Christian Pineau.

U.S. News & World Report. 40:44-5. Ap. 6, '56. Strange war in Algeria.

U.S. News & World Report. 40:46-8+. Ap. 6, '56. France tells allies: "change your attitude"; interview. Guy Mollet.

U.S. News & World Report. 41:53-6. D. 7, '56. Storm over foreign policy: Britain . . . France . . . at home.

United Nations Review. 3:41-3. Ag. '56. Security Council decides not to consider the Algerian question.

United Nations World. 7:8-12+. Ag. '53. Cabal that rules France. G. W. Herald.

United States Department of State Bulletin. 26:895-7. Je. 9, '52. Treaty establishing European defense community signed; statement by Secretary Acheson; with texts of protocol to North Atlantic Treaty, and U.S.-U.K.-French declaration.

United States Department of State Bulletin. 26:931-3. Je. 16, '52. Bonn agreements and the European defense treaty; address, June 2, 1952. D. G. Acheson.
    Same with title Alliance for peace. Vital Speeches of the Day. 18:543-4. Je. 15, '52.

United States Department of State Bulletin. 28:773-7. Je. 1, '53. U.S. objectives in Western Europe. R. B. Knight.

United States Department of State Bulletin. 28:799-804. Je. 8, '53. Launching the European coal and steel community. Raymond Vernon.

United States Department of State Bulletin. 30:747-50. My. 17, '54. Importance of the European defense community to the free world; address. H. C. Lodge, Jr.

United States Department of State Bulletin. 31:13-14. Jl. 5, '54. French friendship for U.S.; text of letter to President Eisenhower, June 23, 1954. René Coty.

United States Department of State Bulletin. 31:719-32. N. 15, '54. Results of Paris conference: texts of the agreements signed at Paris on October 23 relating to NATO.

United States Department of State Bulletin. 35:125. Jl. 16, '56. U.S. views on consideration of Algerian question. H. C. Lodge, Jr.

University of Chicago Round Table. 803:1-17. Ag. 30, '53. Dilemmas of France. Carter Davidson and others.

University of Chicago Round Table. 810:1-18. O. 18, '53. Problems facing France. Herman Finer and Maurice Schumann.

University of Chicago Round Table. 867:1-18. N. 21, '54. France and the future of Europe. Raymond Aron and others.

*Virginia Quarterly Review. 29:321-38. Summer '53. New look at an old ally: the state of France. Gordon Wright.

Vital Speeches of the Day. 19:452-5. My. 15, '53. Unity of Europe, an act of peace; address, April 15, 1953. René Pleven.

Vital Speeches of the Day. 20:40-7. N. 1, '53. France, the key to European peace; address. Maurice Schumann.

Vital Speeches of the Day. 20:205-9. Ja. 15, '54. Continental Europe once more at the crossroads. Karl Brandt.

Vital Speeches of the Day. 22:584-5. Jl. 15, '56. Loyalty to friendships; an address before the National Press Club, Washington, D.C., on June 20, 1956. Christian Pineau.

Western Political Quarterly. 8:186-98. Je. '55. French North Africa: an American problem. L. H. Hahn.

World. p8-13+. F. '54. Is France falling apart? David Schoenbrun.

World Affairs Interpreter. 26:90-100. Ap. '55. French North Africa: a diplomatic dilemma. L. H. Hahn.

World Today. 10:420-9. O. '54. France's problems after the rejection of E.D.C.

World Today. 11:164-73. Ap. '55. Unrest in French North Africa.

World Today. 11:509-18. D. '55. French North African crisis.

Yale French Studies. no 15:3-128. '55. Social and political France [entire issue].

*Yale Review. 44, no 1:64-80. Autumn '54. Twilight of French foreign policy. E. S. Furniss, Jr.

DATE DUE